AGING IN PLACE

James J. Callahan, Jr., Editor

GENERATIONS AND AGING SERIES

Originally published as the Spring 1992 issue of GENERATIONS, Journal of the American Society on Aging, Mary Johnson, Editor.

Baywood Publishing Company, Inc.
Amityville, New York

HV
1461
,A543
1993

Library of Congress Catalog Number: 92-41721
ISBN: 0-89503-113-2

Library of Congress Cataloging-in-Publication Data

Aging in place / James J. Callahan, Jr., editor.
     p.   cm. – – (Generations and aging series)
  "Originally published as the spring 1992 issue of Generations,
journal of the American Society on Aging."
  Includes bibliographical references.
  ISBN 0-89503-113-2 (paper) : $13.95
  1. Aged– –Care– –United States. 2. Aged– –Home care– –United States.
3. Aged– –Housing– –United States. 4. Aged– –United States– –Social
networks.   I. Callahan, James J. II. Series.
HV1461.A543 1993
362.6'1'0973—dc20   92-41721
                                                     CIP

Table of Contents

Chapter 1

Introduction: Aging in Place

James J. Callahan, Jr.

"Aging in place" is among the newer terms to be included along with "senior citizen," "golden agers," "greedy geezers" and others in the lexicon of gerontology. Since aging is a lifelong process and each of us occupies three-dimensional space, we are, of course, always aging in place, but two factors have caused aging in place to emerge as a salient concern for gerontological policy makers. The first is the explosive growth of homeownership after World War II, illustrated in Figure 1. The other is the perception that thousands of older people have been flowing into nursing homes unnecessarily when they can and should remain in their own home or apartment.

The expansion of homeownership was a policy-generated event designed to stimulate the economy after the return of peace. Insured mortgages, deductions of property taxes and mortgage interest, and massive investment in roads and infrastructure served to make owning one's own home a possibility for millions of families and individuals. The suburban sprawl that resulted has made "aging in place" a less than satisfactory situation for many elders by isolating them through lack of transportation, encumbering them with expensive home repairs and routine upkeep, and raising the cost to providers of delivering in-home supportive services.

There were arguments raised against large-scale homeownership during the late thirties. In 1938, Chase argued that homeownership limited job mobility, saddled families with expensive home repairs, and subjected residents to real estate speculation. His answer was the construction of well-managed rental property. Homeownership, however, took off, and now 75 percent of all older persons own their homes—83 percent, mortgage free. Such homeownership does root older people, as Phyllis Mutschler describes in this volume. While 4.5 percent of all elders move yearly (compared to 20 percent of nonelders),

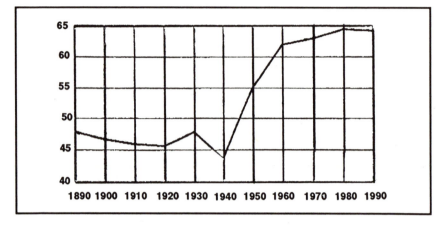

Figure 1. Owner-Occupied Units as a Percentage
of All Occupied Housing Units

only 2 percent of elderly homeowners move compared to 9 percent of nonelders. As for suburbia, Chase did not anticipate all the problems—or their potential solutions—as Pat Hare has done in his article on suburbia's redesign. Hare argues that ability to drive should be an activity of daily living, mini-malls should be created to reduce isolation, and roads and walkways need to be designed to "calm" traffic flows. You will think differently about suburbia after reading Hare.

Contrary to popular perceptions, older persons are not flowing into nursing homes. John Morris and Shirley Morris note that in a given year fewer than one in five elders at high risk of institutionalization will enter a nursing home, remaining at home "largely because of the good efforts of their relatives and friends." Community living is highly valued by most older persons and is the location of choice. Nevertheless, the popular argument continues that the community is the alternative to the institution, and cost offsets must be identified to justify the expansion of community programs. Few informed policy makers, however, now accept this logic.

A look at aging in place must include both the older person and the residential setting. In this volume, Barry Fogel discusses the psychology of aging in place, noting that the meaning of place will vary among individuals and couples. Gender, personality, and personal history all shape a person's orientation to place. The psychological structure of an individual—rather than the physical space itself—may in fact create the "place." Fogel warns against neglecting the subjective dimension of housing because to do so may render a person "homeless"—even with a roof still over his or her head.

Most older persons have families, and as Morris and Morris describe, it is the family system that supports highly disabled elders. Barbara Silverstone and Amy Horowitz expand on this theme and discuss the important issue of autonomy within the context of the family. They raise the very important and still unanswered question, What sacrifices should families be expected to make so that an older person can exercise autonomy and choose to age in place?

Jon Pynoos, Beverley Hynes-Grace, Leah Dobkin, and Susan Lanspery each discuss the setting. Like Chase, Pynoos observes the problems of home maintenance and modification. He reports on a survey of 300 home repair programs and how they operate to help older persons with their homes. He calls for promoting universal design, creative methods of financing, and the passage of a national home modification program.

Beverley Hynes-Grace presents a model of universal design, Hartford House, which offers many innovative features aimed at enhancing the quality of an older person's life. One would hope that dissemination of this model will lead to widespread adaptation of its features.

Elders may want to age in place, but not just any place will do. There are numerous vacancies in senior housing around the country, and many residential communities are waiting to reach capacity. Dobkin reports on AARP's survey of senior housing and warns that housing developers had better know what people want before building, as consumer preferences guide consumer decisions.

Some housing developments were built assuming either perpetual 60-year-olds or outflows of frail elders to family or nursing homes. But elders don't want to leave their apartments any more than they want to leave their houses. The result is that more frail elders are living in "independent" housing. Susan Lanspery reports on a Robert Wood Johnson project that developed a new model of supportive services in senior housing, funded by both housing developers and consumers. Judith Feder, William Scanlon, and Julia Howard report on their evaluation of the program, which is both favorable and hopeful.

Both person and setting are different in rural areas. Ted Koff describes the unique aspects of rural aging, particularly the outflow of resources and people. He argues for rural equity, noting that just as mail is delivered in rural areas at a higher cost than in the city, so should other services available in the city be provided to rural elders. Will Hubbard describes a program in Appalachia that replaces outhouses with indoor plumbing to enable rural inhabitants to age in place.

All may not be well, however, in the cities either. John Skinner reports on the problems faced by African Americans who are poorer and have fewer neighborhood resources than whites. Residential segregation has limited their ability to move, while gentrification has forced them to move against their will, thus disrupting their support system. These problems are compounded by aging and severely restrict choice of living arrangements.

Pat Cullinane describes a program to turn America's aging neighborhoods into support systems for elders while Lori Andersen describes a specific example, the Bay Area Independent Elders Program.

Everyone who will become 65 over the next 30 years is alive today and is being influenced by what they see happening to the aged. The human being's dual capacities for self-interest and foresight are operative. Most of the solutions to the problems of aging in place will be the result of informed decision-making by millions of individuals and couples rather than by either federal or state government officials. Margaret Clemons, a former high-level state policy maker in aging, relates her experience as the daughter of a self-directed aging mother. Mary Sit describes how Rosemary and Gunnar Dybwad anticipated the approach of old age and modified their home environment to satisfy their requirements for prolonged independence.

Individual decisions, however, are aided and abetted by public policy choices on income assistance, housing programs, service systems, and tax code provisions. A society cannot afford to age in place. It must be responsive, and the growing elderly population will challenge both citizens and government. But as Morris and Morris observe, those with an attitude of gloom and doom fail to recognize the varied environmental and service systems spawned by our federal-state governmental partnership and the resiliency of the population once it is mobilized. So, get mobilized for successful aging in place.

* * *

James J. Callahan, Jr., is currently acting dean of the Heller School at Brandeis University, has served as commissioner of the Massachusetts Department of Mental Health and secretary of the commonwealth's Department of Elder Affairs, and is the recipient of the Gerontological Society of America's 1991 Pollack Award for excellence in bridging the worlds of research and practice.

REFERENCES

Chase, S. 1938. "The Case Against Home Ownership." *Survey Graphic*, 27(5)(May):261–67.

New South Wales Government, "Programs for People." Statement by John Hannaford, Minister for Health and Community Services on the 1991–92 NSW Budget.

Chapter 2

Where Elders Live

Phyllis H. Mutschler

Many studies document the remarkable stability of elders' desires regarding housing choices: Elders choose to live independently and remain where they are (Howell, Lane and Friedman, 1982; Boersch-Supan, 1989; Boersch-Supan, Kotlikoff and Morris, 1988) rather than to move in with children or other relatives. Some among the young-old relocate to areas with mild weather when they retire, but, according to Howell and colleagues, fewer than three out of 10 elders considered moving in response to retirement, widowhood, or an "empty nest," and fewer still actually relocated. Relocation was particularly unlikely among elders who were homeowners, and they were less likely to move than were homeowners of other ages. The *American Housing Survey* of 1985 (U.S. Department of Commerce, 1985), for instance, showed that while only 2 percent of elderly homeowners moved, 9 percent of households headed by homeowners of all ages moved in that year (see Table 1).

People of any age often want to remain in their homes for many understandable reasons. Among the strongest are comfort and familiarity with surroundings and the existence of a nearby informal support network. Moreover, elders may want to retain eligibility for available services, which in some cases may be compromised if the elder moves. For instance, elders who sell their homes lose an asset that is excluded in determining eligibility for some forms of income transfer, housing, health, or supportive services programs and replace it with assets that are included in eligibility calculations. Such people

5

Table 1. Home Ownership and Residential Relocation of All U.S. Households
and Households Containing an Elder in 1985
(in thousands)

	Owned by Householder	Rented by Householder
All Households		
N = 88,425	N = 56,145 (64%)	N = 32,280 (36%)
Moved Previous Year N = 17,103 (20%)	4,815	12,288
Became Renter	190	11,158
Became Owner	4,265	1,130
Elderly Households		
N = 18,896 (21%)	N = 13,835[a] (73%)	N = 5,062[a] (27%)
Moved Previous Year N = 855 (4,5%)	318	537
Became Renter[b]	25	517
Became Owner	293	20

Source: *American Housing Survey for the United States in1985.* U.S. Department of Commerce, Current Housing Reports H-150-85. Washington, D.C.
[a]25% of owner households are elderly, as are 16% of renter households.
[b]Only 2% of elderly homeowning households moved, and of those relocating, only 8% moved to rental units. Eleven percent of renting households moved, 96% to another rental unit.

may thereby be rendered ineligible for assistance. Or, a move from a housing development may mean that services provided at that location are lost. Relocation across state borders may also endanger service receipt, since programs vary significantly from state to state.

Thus, the choice to age in place or somewhere else is a function of elders' resources and needs and the range of programs, services, and settings available. Public policy affects these factors through the tax system and public expenditures for programs and transfers, through regulatory activities, and through incentives provided to stimulate or discourage private sector initiatives. Policy interventions occur not only at the federal level but also within the state and localities in which elders reside, and there is wide variation in housing choices and services available to elders in different locations. Other chapters in this volume address these matters more fully, but first it will be useful to review where elders currently reside, the types of dwellings they occupy, and how residence—in particular, housing—affects access to assistance.

GEOGRAPHIC DISTRIBUTION

Although the reasons are still being analyzed (Golant, 1979; Crown and Leavitt, 1988), the fact is that elderly households are unevenly distributed throughout the country. More than one-third of the 18.9 million elderly-occupied dwellings in the United States are found in the South (35%), while fewer than one in five (17%) are in the West (U.S. Department of Commerce, 1985). Three-quarters of the dwellings are classified as urban (with almost one-third located in central cities), and the remaining one-quarter are rural.

OWNER-OCCUPIED DWELLINGS

Three-quarters of all elders own their homes, most (83%) debt-free. In 1985, the median value of these homes was $52,300 (Public Policy Research Associates, Inc., 1989). Among *frail* elderly *homeowners*, nearly all occupy detached houses (84%) or duplexes (5%), but small numbers also live in mobile homes (5%)[1] or apartments (4%) (see Tables 2 and 3). Thus, while "homeownership" commonly connotes residence in a single-family dwelling, it should be noted that other types of residence may also be owned. Conversely, single-family houses and duplexes may also be rented; indeed, one-third of frail elderly renters occupied detached houses (22%) or duplexes (12%).[2]

Because of its symbolic nature and the rights it may confer, owning a home may reinforce the wish to remain "in place." Property ownership, historically the basis for franchise, weighs heavily in a person's sense of worth and personal control. Venti and Wise (1989) report that except for those who have very low incomes and high housing wealth,

---

[1]Mobile homes will be discussed in the section on renter-occupied dwellings because, while owner-occupied mobile homes differ little from other owned units when they sit on property owned by the elders, when the mobile home site is rented, other factors must be considered, whether the mobile home itself is rented or not.

[2]Author's tabulations of National Long Term Care Survey, 1982.

Table 2. Ownership of Dwelling and Dwelling Type
Occupied by Frail Elders
(in thousands)

Dwelling	Owned by Household Member	Rented for Cash	Rented Without Payment	No Information on Owner
Totals 5,054	3,556	1,288	193	17
	(%)	(%)	(%)	(%)
Detached House (N = 3,412)	84	22	72	57
Duplex or Row Home (N = 342)	5	12	4	5
Apartment (N = 933)	4	61	9	23
Room in Hotel (N = 20)	0	1	0	0
Room in Boarding House or Private House (N = 13)	0	1	1	0
Permanent Trailer (N = 199)	5	1	6	7
Mobile Home (N = 106)	2	1	4	6
Other (N = 27)	0	1	4	3
Totals	100%	100%	100%	100%

Source: Author's tabulations of the National Long Term Care Survey, 1982.
Note: Percentages may add to more than 100% because of rounding. Frailty is defined as requiring assistance with at least one activity of daily living or instrumental activity of daily living for a period of at least three months.

Table 3. Ownership of Dwelling by Elderly Householder's Level of Frailty
(in thousands)

	Mild 1 IADL No ADL (N =1,938)	Low Moderate 4+ IADL No ADL (N = 364)	High Moderate 1–2 ADL 0–8 IADL (N = 364)	Severe 3+ ADL 0–8 IADL (N = 957)	Total (N =5,054)
	(%)	(%)	(%)	(%)	(%)
Dwelling Owned by Household Member (N = 3,560)	38	7	35	20	100
Dwelling Rented for Cash (N = 1,292)	40	7	36	17	100
Dwelling Rented Without Payment of Rent (N = 194)	33	7	43	17	100
No Information On Ownership (N = 28)	35	8	35	22	100

Source: Author's tabulation of 1982 National Long Term Care Survey.

the transaction costs (including psychic costs) of moving or reducing equity are too high for relocation or reverse annuity mortgages to be considered attractive.

Beyond these motives, favorable tax treatment of certain housing costs or of modifications that aid independent living, as well as local policies granting property tax relief, provide incentives for continued homeownership. These and other public policies currently reinforce elders' desire to stay in the family home. Moreover, since the asset value of a home represents most of elders' wealth, it is a source of financial security and a means to bequeath wealth to their heirs.

When elders remain in single-family homes, however, service delivery can be more costly, particularly if they are at some distance

Table 4. Advantages and Disadvantages of Selected Alternative Housing Options

	Advantages	Disadvantages
Accessory Apartments	• provide additional income for elderly homeowners • companionship and security • increase supply of affordable rental housing • personal support services may be provided in lieu of rent	• initial construction cost to homeowners • neighborhood concern about lowered property values • zoning restraints • possible housing and building code violations
Board and Care Homes	• homelike environment • afford fragile, isolated elderly opportunity to interact with others • economical	• not licensed or concerned with standards and treatment of residents • owner/operators often lack training • little planned social activities
Congregate Housing	• provides basic support services that can extend independent living • reduces social isolation • provides physical and emotional security	• tendency to overserve the need of tenants, promoting dependency • expensive to build and operate • those without kitchen facilities restrict tenants independence • expensive for most elderly without subsidy
Elder Cottages. Granny Flats	• facilitate older persons receiving support from younger family members • option to remain in individual home • smaller housing unit, less expensive to operate	• potential to lower property values • attitude of and impact on neighborhood • concerns about housing and building code violations

	Advantages	Disadvantages
Home Equity Conversion	• converts lifetime investment into usable income • allows elderly with marginal incomes to remain in familiar surroundings • can be used to finance housing expenses, i.e., make necessary repairs, utilities, taxes	• risk that homeowner will live longer than term of loan • homes of lower value (often type owned by elderly) may not provide monthly payments large enough to be worth cost of loan • reluctance by homeowner to utilize due to lack of information, concern for lien on property, and/or impact on estate for heirs
Life Care Facilities	• offer prepaid healthcare • security and protection against inflation and financially draining illness • wide range of social activities with health and support systems	• too expensive for many elderly • questionable protections should the facility go out of business • older person receives no deed to property • location that monthly payments will not rise • location is usually rural, isolated from community services
Shared Housing	• less expensive due to shared costs for household operators • companionship, security • promotes intergenerational cooperation and understanding • more extensive use of existing housing • program inexpensive to operate	• problems with selection of individual to share home • amount of privacy reduced • does not meet medical and personal problems • added income may mean owner is no longer eligible for public benefits • city zoning ordinances may prohibit

Source: Adapted from *A Manual of Housing Alternatives for the Elderly, Vol. I*, Rosalyn Katz, Ph.D., Health and Welfare Planning Association for the City of Pittsburgh, and *Housing Choices for Older Homeowners*, American Association of Retired Persons. Prepared by West Virginia Commission on Aging.

from others who need similar services. And some argue that frail elders in single-family dwellings, particularly if they live alone, are more likely to become isolated and thus receive less adequate care than those who live in congregate facilities. On the other hand, when homes are owned, modifications and repairs can be undertaken without consulting a landlord or supervisory body, and accessory apartments that provide extra income or a place for caretakers to live are also more easily arranged.

RENTER-OCCUPIED DWELLINGS

Although the majority of elders reside in single-family dwellings or apartments that they own, elderly renters occupy more than 5 million dwellings (U.S. Department of Commerce, 1985, Table 7-9). Nearly all nonhomeowning elders (85%) rent their dwellings for cash; the rest do not pay rent. More than six out of 10 renters live in apartments, but as noted earlier, one-third occupy detached or "row" houses.

Because there are no standard categories of dwellings for elders who do not own homes, it is difficult to identify how many people live in a particular type of domicile. For example, the Bureau of the Census uses the following categories: house, apartment or flat, unit in a nontransient hotel, unit in a transient hotel, unit in a rooming house, and mobile home. The National Long Term Care Survey utilizes slightly different categories, which, along with the number of renters in each, are found in Table 2.

Elderly renters differ in important ways from elderly homeowners: The median age of renters is more than two years greater, and they are more likely to be female and to spend a greater proportion of their income on shelter. A disproportionate number of African American elders are renters. However, they are underrepresented in federally assisted housing, raising questions about intentional or de facto admission bias (Pastalan, 1985). More than half of elderly renters had excessive expenditures for housing, compared with 30 percent of all elders (U.S. Department of Commerce, 1985). Consequently, renters are more likely than owners to be limited in the ways they can modify their dwelling to accommodate increased disability or to enhance caregiving. Since strikingly similar proportions of elderly homeowners and renters are severely disabled in carrying out activities of daily living (see Table 3), renters are likely to be disadvantaged. The problems and opportunities faced by elderly renters in these dwellings—apartments, trailers, rooms, board and care homes, and other arrangements—with respect to long-term care are discussed below.

Apartments

Apartments are the second largest category of housing and the largest category of rented dwellings occupied by the elderly, with most elders likely to live in buildings containing more than five units.[3] Rent may be paid privately or through public subsidies. Apartments may be located in mixed-generation developments or in developments primarily for the elderly. Apartments offer some advantages such as the security of neighbors in close proximity and the need for less maintenance, particularly out of doors. Services such as window washing and storm window hanging may be included in the rent for some buildings. Building requirements associated with some developments, elevators and dining areas, for example, can assist frail elders to remain in those dwellings.

However, apartment dwellers may face a number of problems. Some, despite low incomes, pay rents that exceed 30 percent of income. Often they cannot renovate or modify their units without obtaining permission from the property manager or landlord. If the owner or building manager is not willing to make changes, or allow them to be made at the tenants' expense, elders with increasing functional limitations may be forced to move.

Many privately owned apartment buildings, although once multigenerational, have become what can be called naturally occurring retirement communities as tenants have aged in place or younger tenants have moved to larger apartments or purchased homes. Those who live in these buildings may be able to obtain services at lower costs because of economies of scale—relatively inexpensive homemaker and

---

[3]The *American Housing Survey* of 1989 shows that almost 4.58 million elderly-headed households live in dwellings designated "multiple units"; the largest number, 1.6 million, live in structures of 2 to 4 units, and another 1.2 million live in structures containing 50 or more units. Of the more than 20 million elderly-headed households, more than 13.31 million are in detached houses, 975,000 in attached houses, and more than 1.23 million in mobile homes. The remainder occupy apartments or rooms in private homes or other residential settings. Estimates from the National Long Term Care Survey (1982) show that of *frail* elders renting their dwellings, 11,000 have rooms in boarding houses, 5,000 rent rooms in private houses, and another 14,000 rent rooms in hotels. "Frail" elders are defined as those who have limitations in performing instrumental activities of daily living, for example, housecleaning, cooking, or shopping.

medical care services through arrangements made by managers, for example.

Accessory apartments and "elder cottages" are two types of apartments receiving recent attention in elderly housing discussions. Accessory apartments are created within an existing single-family home and provide the opportunity for exchanging services and generating income. Elder cottages (also referred to as Elder Cottage Housing Opportunities or ECHO) are prefabricated small dwellings that may be physically set apart from a house on a single site, typically a family member's or other caregiver's lot (Hare and Hollis, 1983); utilities are drawn from the "host" house. Like accessory apartments, ECHO units offer caregiving opportunities that allow an elderly person to remain independent, but with support nearby. However, unlike accessory apartments, ECHO units can be moved when the occupant dies or leaves and are often inexpensive to build.[4] Both arrangements often have to overcome zoning restrictions: An elder cottage technically reduces lot size, while accessory apartments cause single family dwellings to be classified as multifamily or business buildings. Perhaps because of such problems, or because these alternatives have not been vigorously promoted, there has been only scant interest in and relatively little development of them.

Mobile homes

Mobile homes, or trailers, are the third-largest category of housing for elders. Almost 1 million households composed of one or two frail or unimpaired elders reside in trailers. Although most mobile homes (85%) are owned by those who live in them, the places in which they are parked are leased; consequently, not all of the advantages enjoyed by other property owners are available to mobile home owners. Mobile homes do offer the advantage of providing limited, manageable living space at lower cost than buildings constructed on foundations. In large parks that cater to elders, there are opportunities to offer services at affordable rates because, as in apartment complexes, economies of scale in service delivery allow lower costs. However, trailer owners and renters confront several problems. For example, trailer parks are often located far from services, and there is no guarantee of permanence if the park is sold (Carroll and Gray, 1985). Costs of moving mobile homes

---

[4]Hare (1987) estimates that the cost of a one bedroom, 528-square-foot unit is $26,635, without shipping.

can be prohibitive—frequently between $30 and $45 per hour for a move.

Rooms

Rooms are the fourth-largest category of housing for elders. They may be rented in private residences or in a motel or hotel, where the latter is referred to as a single room occupancy (SRO) unit (defined by HUD as a partial room lacking a complete and private kitchen or plumbing facilities and housed in a building of at least 12 similar units). Although they have received less attention than public housing units, SROs may have housed more people, and while the quality of SRO rooms and the buildings in which they are located is often below standard, the low rents and access to inner city services make them a viable—in some cases the only—alternative to homelessness for most of the residents (Minkler and Ovrebo, 1985). In addition, some SROs provide informal support through neighbors or managers, and because elders are in one location, the potential exists for cost-effective service delivery. Since the early 1980s, urban apartment building conversions and renovations have drastically reduced the numbers of SRO residents.

Board and Care

The 1976 Keys Amendment to the Housing Act defines a board and care home as a nonmedical facility that provides room, board, and some protective oversight for residents. Protective oversight may be as limited as knowing the resident's whereabouts or as extensive as providing assistance with activities of daily living. Although exact figures are not known, between 50,000 and 100,000 people over age 65 are residing in facilities referred to as adult homes or boarding homes (U.S. House of Representatives, 1989).[5] Over 40 percent of such homes

[5]Reliable estimates of the number of elders residing in board and care facilities are difficult to obtain. An AARP report of a 1987 survey conducted by the National Association of Residential Care Facilities identified 41,000 faculties housing 563,000 residents. Likewise, Newcomer and Stone (1985) report that "a 1983 study of state board and care licensing programs estimated 458,000 board and care beds nationally with 324,000 beds for the aged or physical disabled." In both these estimates, elderly residents represent only a fraction of the total numbers of individuals in these facilities. Most observers believe that between 1.5 percent and 2.5 percent of elderly live in board and care homes. Based on estimates from the National Long Term Care Survey, these proportions led us to estimates reported here.

are not licensed, although the federal government pays more than $3 billion in Supplemental Security Income to residents (Capitman, 1987), who then pay for their room, board, and protective oversight. States often provide additional subsidies for special populations (e.g., those who are mentally ill), and such funds may be required if these units are to be made available to poor or near-poor frail elders.

At their best, board and care homes offer a secure, noninstitutional home for elders with moderate disabilities. However, there are many reports of abuse by board and care operators and of building deficiencies. Investigations of such abuses have led members of the Select Committee on Aging's Subcommittee on Long-Term Care to recommend increased homecare services to make it easier for individuals to avoid moving to a board and care home (U.S. House of Representatives, 1989). Other policy options include more stringent regulation of board and care homes, physical structures, and operator qualifications.

A particular form of board and care available in many parts of the country is adult foster care, in which small numbers of frail elders and other disabled adults are cared for in the home of an unrelated individual. In the state of Oregon, for example, a major initiative has been undertaken to divert elders from nursing homes and larger board and care facilities to licensed foster care homes. The operators of the residences must also be licensed and are required to receive training as nurses or nursing aides. Oregon Administrative Rule 41-50-443 limits the number of bed-bound individuals in any one dwelling and requires that the resident's placement be reassessed twice yearly. At its best, foster care contributes both to elders' sense of independence and security—since operators are trained to encourage them to care for themselves as much as possible—while also providing assistance that is needed along with the required "oversight." If, however, the state budget fails to keep pace with the number of foster care homes and enforcement of regulations becomes lax, operator qualifications and resident assessments may not be sufficient to ensure independence and security.

Other Housing Arrangements

Apartments, rooms, and mobile homes are the primary housing options for low-income elderly persons who do not own homes. Other alternatives for higher-income elders are often referred to as retirement communities and are characterized by contractual arrangements either for housing only or for housing and additional features and services such as communal buildings, organized social activities, and various kinds of support. Pastalan (1985) describes five kinds of retirement communities, each of which is the residential choice of over a million elders. These communities range from new towns, smaller villages, or subdivisions designed specifically for elders to multiunit apartment buildings, cooperatives, or condominiums that are age-segregated.

One specialized retirement community receiving increasing attention is the continuing care retirement community. These communities of apartment or town-house structures offer both independent living arrangements and nursing home beds on the same campus, with nursing home care a part of the contract. Many include an intermediate, assisted living facility as well. The contracts may also include housekeeping and meal plans that enhance independence (Pastalan, 1985). Although research into the costs of operating continuing care retirement communities is just beginning, current contracts require entry and monthly fees beyond the reach of many elderly.

SUMMARY

Each of these settings offers opportunities for frail elders to sustain independent living, but none is ideal. Table 4 summarizes the major advantages and disadvantages of the main settings and program types. Those that offer a comprehensive package of services are either in short supply or too costly for most elders who need them. In addressing the long-term-care needs of elders, we must not ignore the ways that homes—owned or rented—can accommodate elders' increasing frailty and provide ease of access to services. Policy makers striving to assist elders to remain in their communities will need to acknowledge the important role played by housing in supporting continued independence among the aged.

*   *   *

Phyllis H. Mutschler, Ph.D., is senior research assistant and lecturer, Policy Center on Aging, Heller School, Brandeis University, Waltham, Mass.

REFERENCES

Boersch-Supan, A., 1989. *A Dynamic Analysis of Household Dissolution and Living Arrangement Transitions by Elderly Americans*. Working Paper No. 2808. Cambridge, Mass.: National Bureau of Economic Research, January.

Boersch-Supan, A., Kotlikoff, L. J. and Morris, J., 1988. *The Dynamics of Living Arrangements of the Elderly*. Working Paper No. 2787. Cambridge, Mass.: National Bureau of Economic Research, December.

Capitman, J. A., 1987. "Present and Future Roles of SSI and Medicaid in Funding Board and Care Homes." Paper prepared for AARP Conference on Board and Care Homes.

Carroll, K. and Gray, V. K., 1985. "Exploding Some Myths About Housing for the Elderly." *Real Estate Review* 15(2): 91–93.

Crown, W. H. and Leavitt, T. D., 1988. *Policy Implications of Elderly Interstate Migration*. Waltham, Mass.: Brandeis University, Policy Center on Aging, October.

Golant, S. M., ed., 1979. *Location and Environment of Elderly Population*. Washington, D.C.: V. H. Winston and Sons.

Hare, P., 1987. *Accessory Apartments and ECHO Units*. Washington, D.C.: Council of State Housing Agencies and the National Association of State Units on Aging.

Hare, P. and Hollis, L., 1983. *ECHO Housing: A Review of Zoning Issues and Other Considerations*. Washington, D.C.: American Association of Retired Persons.

Howell, S., Lane, T. S. and Friedman, S., 1982. *Determinants of Housing Choice Among the Elderly*. Unpublished paper. Department of Health and Human Services, Administration on Aging Grant No. AR-2116/01, March.

Minkler, M. and Ovrebo, B., 1985. "SROs." *Generations* 11 (3): 40–42.

Pastalan, L. A., 1985. "Retirement Communities." *Generations* 11 (3): 26–30.

Public Policy Research Associates, Inc., 1989. *The Public Policy and Aging Report* (Jan/Feb).

U.S. Department of Commerce, 1985. *American Housing Survey for the United States in 1985*. Current Housing Reports H-150-85, 305-313. Washington, D.C.

U.S. House of Representatives, 1989. *Board and Care Homes in America: A National Tragedy*. Select Committee on Aging, 101th Cong., 1st Sess., Comm. Pub. No. 101-711. Washington, D.C.: Government Printing Office.

Venti, S. F. and Wise, D. A., 1989. *But They Don't Want to Reduce Housing Equity*. Working Paper No. 2859. Cambridge, Mass.: National Bureau of Economic Research, February.

Chapter 3

Psychological Aspects of Staying at Home

Barry S. Fogel

Older people are less mobile than younger people and often choose to stay in their houses or apartments despite apparent economic or health-related reasons for moving. Economic studies of housing wealth in the elderly suggest that houses are not treated as mere economic assets (Borsch-Supan, 1990; Venti and Wise, 1990) but as objects of emotional attachment. Abundant clinical anecdotes describe older people who refuse to move, despite the conviction of clinicians and relatives that a move would be in their best interest.

While the general tendency of older people to remain in place is well established, individuals differ greatly in their willingness to move and in the specific reasons for their attachment to their homes. Understanding these individual differences is relevant both to the design of housing for the elderly and to planning clinical interventions with people who object to moves that may be desirable for social, medical, or financial reasons. Moreover, aging individuals' better understanding of the nature of their attachment to their homes can be helpful in planning for moves and living arrangements later in life.

This chapter will discuss some of the psychological benefits older people derive from living in their homes and some of the factors that influence the relevance of particular benefits for particular people. People may or may not be consciously aware of the benefits of their home. Dramatically negative responses to moving can occur in people who have minimized the benefits of their previous residence or have been unaware of them.

In all of this discussion, the term "home" refers to a residence that a person has occupied for several years, be it owned or rented, a house or an apartment. A separate section later in the chapter will discuss the issue of institutions as "homes."

BENEFITS OF HOME

Benefits of home comprise several categories: (1) benefits related to independence, such as privacy and control over physical features of the home environment (Lawton, 1985; Golant, 1984; Rubinstein, 1989; McCartney, 1988); (2) benefits related to familiarity of a particular home environment, for example, ease of finding one's way around (Rowles, 1987); (3) benefits related to residence in a specific neighborhood, including a social network of friends and neighbors (Antonucci and Akiyama, 1991; Arling, 1976; Rowles, 1987), and access to community services; (4) benefits related to the activities of home maintenance, as a source of physical and mental exercise and as a source of meaning (Herzog and House, 1991); (5) benefits related to the home as a place to entertain friends and family, to reciprocate hospitality, and to pursue avocational activities (Rubinstein, 1989); and (6) benefits related to the home as a locus of meaning—the site of important and memorable life events (Danermark and Ekstrom, 1990; Rubinstein, 1989). Homeowners may enjoy the further benefit of their home as a status symbol (Rowles, 1987) and tangible asset (Cutler and Gregg, 1991).

Over and above these considerations, some people appear to feel attached to their homes much as they would feel attached to a significant person—their love transcends any rational calculation of benefit. They can enumerate reasons why a move would be wise but then conclude that the only way they would leave their home would be in a box.

INDIVIDUAL DIFFERENCES IN THE MEANING OF HOME

The particular psychological aspects of staying home most important to particular individuals are likely to depend on gender, socioeconomic status, health status, and marital status. In general, women are more likely than men to be concerned with preserving their neighborhood social networks—the loss of proximity to friends and neighbors may be the major problem with moving. Women may feel differently about possessions than do men, with women tending to be more attached to memorabilia and men to items of instrumental value, such as furniture and appliances. Furthermore, elderly women spend more time at home than do elderly men and therefore may be more affected by their home environments (Danermark and Ekstrom, 1990).

People of higher socioeconomic status are more likely to own houses and be able to afford structural modifications that suit their own tastes and needs. People are more likely to become attached to a building they have designed, built, or remodeled. On the other hand, people of higher status are more likely to be in good health and to engage in activities outside the home (Schank and Lough, 1987). For more active people, the neighborhood, rather than the home itself, may have greater importance.

Health status, including functional status, has profound effects on the meaning of home. Litwak and Longino (1987) emphasized in their model of migration in the elderly that healthy, functional older people tend to move in pursuit of amenities and in order to facilitate their avocational interests. Migration of functionally impaired and unhealthy elderly is more likely to be motivated by the need to be near supportive services or caregiving family members (Longino et al., 1991). Parallel differences apply to the psychological meaning of the home itself. For healthy and highly functional people, attachment to home often emphasizes the social and physical characteristics of the neighborhood. Among more impaired people, independence and autonomy loom larger as reasons for attachment to home. Rubinstein (1989) has beautifully described how functionally impaired older people can organize their personal space to conserve energy and maximize both autonomy and meaning. For the more impaired, remaining at home may have the additional significance of being the one constant in an emotional world threatened by losses.

People with impaired cognition can show measurably better intellectual function when tested at home (Ward et al., 1990). While this observation may simply reflect lower anxiety and less distraction in the home setting, it is tempting to speculate that individuals with failing cognition do better when no energy must be expended on coping with a new and different environment. Dramatic differences in performance at home and in the clinic would not be expected from higher-functioning people.

Marital status is also associated with differences in the psychological significance of home. For many married people, home is where their spouse is; the presence of a living spouse makes a change in residence less psychologically threatening. However, it is not uncommon for spouses to disagree about their ideal living environment, so it may happen that the death of a spouse leaves a survivor free to live where he or she has preferred to live all along.

HOME MAINTENANCE AS A BURDEN

As any homeowner knows, the repair and maintenance of a house can be both time-consuming and costly. Home repair and maintenance constituted the predominant unpaid economic activity of older people studied by Herzog and House (1991). As health problems and functional impairments accumulate, the effort involved in household maintenance would be expected to become greater and more burdensome. In a recent study of residents of subsidized elderly housing in Rhode Island, the author and his colleagues found that many elderly with incomes of less than $12,500 per year were willing to pay $7.00 an hour for housecleaning.

For many elderly, however, the solution is neither to move nor to hire help, but simply to maintain the home less well or to restrict themselves to a smaller part of the house or apartment. Thus, while maintaining a home becomes increasingly effortful with failing health, the psychological advantages of staying in place outweigh the potential convenience of a different residence that would be smaller or would include some maintenance and support services.

The literature on coping in the elderly suggests that passive strategies involving emotional accommodation rather than external action are preferred by the current cohort of elderly (Folkman et al., 1987). The substantial planning, anticipation, and activity involved in a residential move are less in accord with the preferred coping strategies of many elderly people than are the emotional adjustments needed to live in a less tidy house or to close off unused rooms.

The perception of home maintenance as a burden is influenced not only by the physical and mental demands of housekeeping but also by the mood state of the resident. Depression, that most common mental disorder of late life, tends to diminish the capacity for effort as well as the pleasure to be derived from the home; at the same time, depressive irritability intensifies the hassles involved in caring for the home, and depressive pessimism promotes the conclusion that things will only get worse in the future. As a consequence, depression can trigger a decision to sell a house, to move closer to relatives, or to give up independent living. Colsher and Wallace (1990), studying a sample of rural community elderly, found a significantly higher level of depressive symptoms at baseline in people who moved during the following year.

The association of depression with the decision to move confounds analyses of the psychological consequences of relocation. A common clinical anecdote concerns the older person who decided to change living arrangements because of depression and then discovered that she had moved out of the frying pan and into the microwave.

THE ROLE OF PERSONALITY

The psychological meaning of home is strongly influenced by personality traits, both normal and pathological. Extroverted individuals may find that the greatest meaning of their homes lies in their neighborhoods and in the home as a site for social interaction. If they must move, however, they are likely to adapt better to new residences because of their greater facility at meeting people. Introverts may be more strongly attached to the physical rather than the social environment of their homes.

Another perspective on personality and attachment to home is offered by the Jungian analyst Jean Bolen. She describes women whose main gratifications come from homemaking and whose archetype is the goddess Hestia. For such women, domestic activities are the primary outlet for their creativity (Bolen, 1984). While there is no precise male equivalent, she describes men whose principal satisfactions come from tinkering with the material world and whose archetype is the god Hephaestus. Such men may take extraordinary pride and satisfaction in household repairs and improvements and in maintaining the yard or garden (Bolen 1989).

Personality styles and personality disorders can strongly influence people's feelings about their homes, and their reactions to a change in residence or living arrangements. The influence of each of several common personality styles on the relationship to home will be discussed briefly.

Compulsive personalities are preoccupied with orderliness and control. For them, retaining control over their personal space is an important reason for remaining at home. Concerns about economy can work in either direction, sometimes favoring a move that might be otherwise unsatisfactory and sometimes opposing a move on grounds of its expense. Deterioration of the house or the neighborhood can be particularly upsetting to compulsive people.

Hysterical personalities may seize upon an emotionally salient aspect of their housing or living arrangements and make decisions based on it without regard to the totality of all relevant information. A person with hysterical traits might decide to move in reaction to a single episode of burglary, not considering the losses and adjustments that might be entailed in the change of residence. Or, the person might choose to remain in a house because of sentimental attachment, despite overwhelming problems in maintaining the residence.

Narcissistic personalities may be intensely concerned about their social status, and may make housing choices based on status considerations. They may choose housing that does not ideally meet their physical and social requirements if such housing is in a sufficiently desirable and prestigious neighborhood or building. They may also have a particularly hard time in making a transition from being owners to being renters or in accepting a congregate or sheltered living arrangement.

People with borderline personalities that are characterized by intense but unstable affect are notorious for changing their minds about housing decisions. Moves can be made with great enthusiasm, followed eventually by intense dissatisfaction when some realistic disappointment arises with the housing, neighborhood, or living arrangements.

People with odd or eccentric personalities, including paranoid and schizoid individuals, may intensely value the privacy and control afforded by living alone. While reluctant to enter into congregate living arrangements, they also often reject supportive services that involve people coming into their homes, because of the loss of privacy and control.

INSTITUTIONS AS HOMES

In visiting very-long-term residents of institutions such as mental hospitals and nursing homes, one is struck by the extent to which some residents truly relate to the facility as their home. Characteristically, these residents have close personal relationships with staff members or with other residents. Often, they have found some way to structure their personal space with decorations or memorabilia. Even when conditions in the institution are far from attractive, such residents are often strikingly reluctant to move in pursuit of improved conditions.

For such people the elements of familiarity and attachment to people outweigh the hassles and discomforts so readily apparent to casual visitors. Moreover, many of these patients experience a higher degree of physical comfort and personal attention in the institutional environment than they knew prior to their admission. This is particularly true for the chronically mentally ill and for people who have struggled alone with severe physical disabilities before their admission to the institution.

Rosalie Kane and her associates (1990) have noted that nursing home residents greatly value their autonomy over the daily details of their existence—matters such as coming and going as they please and access to the telephone. Privacy also is highly valued. Institutions offering privacy and autonomy are very desirable places for functionally impaired elderly who must give up their own homes because of incapacity. However, people can regard institutions as "home" even when privacy and autonomy are lacking.

As with feelings about private residences, the capacity to experience an institution as one's home varies enormously among individuals. More passive and dependent people have an easier time accepting and even enjoying institutional life than those for whom activity and independence are central issues.

SECOND HOMES

While second homes are a luxury enjoyed by only a minority of the population, enough older people do have vacation homes, summer or winter residences, to warrant a comment on their special psychological meanings.

First, summer or winter homes enable people to defer decisions about leaving a primary residence in a place with an unpleasant climate in one season of the year. As long as the effort to maintain a second residence is not too overwhelming and travel not too difficult, the second home enables people to hold on to attachments to friends and neighbors who continue to live in the area of their primary residence.

Second, vacation homes often have been the site of particularly happy experiences, including family reunions, vacations, and enjoyable times spent alone with a spouse. For this reason, they may symbolize the good things in life disproportionately to the time spent there.

Third, second homes may be an ongoing locus for family reunions and more attractive to children and grandchildren than the primary residence. For all these reasons, older people may experience definite feelings of loss and grief when giving up a second home, even when their primary residence is maintained. Specific feelings will be modified by individual personality. For some people, the emotional attachment to the second home is greater than the attachment to the primary residence.

IMPLICATIONS FOR CAREGIVERS

The central idea of this chapter is that people's attachments to their homes may be as intense and as complex as their attachments to friends and relatives and are influenced by personality and mood in much the same way. Yet, housing decisions frequently are made in the press of clinical circumstances, with far less thought than would be applied, for example, to a marital separation. Both family and professional caregivers at times underestimate the psychological meaning of the home, because of their focus on physical security and medical needs. The consequences, often demoralizing, are sometimes avoidable.

Efforts at preventing unwise housing decisions must begin with efforts to anticipate changes in residence and to talk about them in a multidimensional fashion. Understanding what aspect of a person's current home means the most to him or her will help in finding the best residential alternative when living at home is no longer feasible. A simple example concerns nursing home choice: Thoughtful care planners know who is likely to care more about the decor of the nursing home and who will care more about autonomy.

The widespread preference of older people (and all people) for some space that they personally control and structure should be considered in the planning of all long-term institutions. Increasingly, the importance of private space is finding its way into the architectural design of nursing homes. Recently, Vallerand, O'Connor and Blais (1989) showed that residents of "high self-determination" nursing homes had levels of life satisfaction comparable to those of community-dwelling elderly and significantly higher than those of residents of "low self-determination" homes. Their five criteria for self-determination were (1) how much choice residents had regarding mealtimes, (2) the extent to which nursing home staff were responsible for residents' personal care, (3) how free residents were to decorate and arrange the furniture in their rooms, (4) whether the residents were allowed to have or care for a pet, and (5) the degree to which staff encouraged or discouraged personal initiative.

In considering the emotional reactions of people who are unhappy after a change of residence or living arrangements, one should weigh both the personal meaning of the residential change to the individual and those mood and personality factors that might be influencing their reaction. At the outset, it is usually best to identify whether there is a practical, remediable issue that would make the new residence more acceptable. However, if there are significant depressive symptoms, these will probably need treatment to enable the person to make the best possible adaptation to the new environment. In this regard, it is important to note the work of Parmelee, Katz and Lawton (1989) who showed that approximately 40 percent of nursing home residents suffer from a clinically significant degree of depression.

CONCLUSION

This chapter has discussed the subjective dimension of older people's attachment to their homes. Attention to these psychological issues is likely to improve resident satisfaction with new models of housing for the elderly. Furthermore, the concerns outlined in this chapter may offer some guidance to clinicians and family members who may wish to better understand an older person's feelings about a possible or recent relocation. Aging people contemplating residential moves might benefit from systematic reflection on the nature of their attachment to their present residence and on their housing-related personal values. Finally, public policy regarding elderly housing and community-based long-term care must not neglect the subjective dimension of housing and must strive for solutions that leave no person "homeless."

* * *

Barry S. Fogel, M.D., is associate director of the Center for Gerontology and Health Care Research and associate professor of psychiatry, Brown University, Providence, R.I.

REFERENCES

Antonucci, T. and Akiyama, H., 1991. "Social Relationships and Aging Well." *Generations* 15 (1):39–44.

Arling, G., 1976. "The Elderly Widow and Her Family, Neighbors and Friends." *Journal of Marriage and the Family* 1976 (November):757–68.

Bolen, J. S., 1984. *Goddesses in Everywoman.* New York: Harper & Row.

Bolen, J. S., 1989. *Gods in Everyman.* New York: Harper & Row.

Borsch-Supan, A., 1990. "Household Dissolution and the Choice of Alternative Living Arrangements Among Elderly Americans." In D. Wise, ed., *Economics of Aging.* Chicago: University of Chicago Press.

Colsher, P. L. and Wallace, R. B., 1990. "Health and Social Antecedents of Relocation in Rural Elderly Persons." *Journal of Gerontology, Social Sciences* 48(1)S32–38.

Cutler, N. E. and Gregg, D. W., 1991. "The Human 'Wealth Span' and Financial Well-Being in Older Age." *Generations* 15(1):45–48.

Danermark, B. and Ekstrom M., 1990. "Relocation and Health Effects on the Elderly: A Commented Research Review." *Journal of Sociology and Social Welfare* 17(1):25–49.

Folkman, S. et al., 1987. "Age Differences in Stress and Coping Processes." *Psychology and Aging* 2(2):171–84.

Golant, M. S., 1984. *A Place to Grow Old*. New York:Columbia University Press.

Herzog, A. R. and House, J. S., 1991. "Productive Activities and Aging Well." *Generations* 15(1):49–54.

Kane, R. L. et al., 1990. "Everyday Autonomy in Nursing Homes." *Generations* 14(Suppl.):86–89.

Lawton, M. P., 1985. "The Elderly in Context: Perspectives from Environmental Psychology and Gerontology." *Environment and Behavior* 17(4):501–19.

Litwak, E. and Longino, C. F., 1987. "Migration Patterns Among the Elderly: A Developmental Perspective." *Gerontologist* 27(3):266–72.

Longino, C. F. et al., 1991. "The Second Move: Health and Geographic Mobility." *Journal of Gerontology, Social Sciences* 48(4):S218–24.

McCartney, J. R., 1988. "Elderly Women Who Want to Live Alone: Lessons Learned." *Journal of Geriatric Psychiatry and Neurology* 1(3):171–74.

Parmelee. P. A., Katz, I. R. and Lawton M. P., 1989. "Depression Among Institutionalized Aged: Assessment and Prevalence Estimation." *Journal of Gerontology* 44(1):M22–29.

Rowles, G. D., 1987. "A Place to Call Home." In L. L. Carstensen and B. A. Edelstein, eds., *Handbook of Clinical Gerontology*. New York: Pergamon Press.

Rubinstein, R. L., 1989. "The Home Environments of Older People: A Description of the Psychosocial Processes Linking Person to Place." *Journal of Gerontology, Social Sciences* 44(2):S45–53.

Schank, M. J. and Lough, M. A., 1987. "Maintaining Health and Independence of Elderly Women." *Journal of Gerontological Nursing* 15(6):8–11.

Vallerand, R. J., O'Connor, B. P. and Blais, M. R., 1989. "Life Satisfaction of Elderly Individuals in Regular Community Housing, in Low-Cost Community Housing, and High and Low Self-Determination Nursing Homes." *International Journal of Aging and Human Development* 28(4):277–83.

Venti, S. F. and Wise, D. A., 1990. "Aging, Moving, and Housing Wealth." In D. Wise, ed., *Economics of Aging*. Chicago: University of Chicago Press.

Ward, H. W. et al., 1990. "Cognitive Function Testing in Comprehensive Geriatric Assessment." *Journal of American Geriatric Society* 38:1088–92.

Chapter 4

Strategies for Home Modification and Repair*

Jon Pynoos

Home modification and repair have emerged as public policy and service delivery issues because they can help older people age in place. When older people become frail, the home environment needs to be *more* supportive to compensate for their limitations or disabilities (Lawton, 1980; Pynoos, 1988; Pynoos, in press; Pynoos et al., 1987). A significant number of the elderly, however, live in housing that has in fact deteriorated, lacks supportive features, or presents barriers to mobility. These types of problems make it difficult to safely carry out activities such as cooking meals, bathing, climbing stairs, reading, or doing housework. In order to increase the incidence of home modification and repair, improvements need to be made in assessing homes, expanding public awareness, and developing programs.

Federal legislation supporting home modifications and repair would greatly enhance these efforts.

PROBLEMS ENCOUNTERED BY THE ELDERLY

Because the elderly tend to live in the oldest parts of the housing stock, their dwelling units are often difficult to maintain. Approximately

*Preparation of this chapter was supported, in part, by grant number 90-AM 0498601, from the Administration on Aging, Department of Health and Human Services. Grantees undertaking projects under government sponsorship are encouraged to express freely their findings and conclusions. Points of view or opinions do not, therefore, necessarily represent official Administration on Aging policy.

6.3 percent of elderly households experience problems such as leaking roofs, inadequate wiring, and poorly functioning plumbing (Mikelsons and Turner, 1991). In addition, elderly households often have inefficient heating and cooling systems and insufficient insulation.

While the overall rate of inadequate housing conditions is low, serious problems exist among particular segments of the elderly population. For example, 4 percent of elderly white owner-households live in moderately to severely inadequate housing, in contrast to 23 percent of elderly black and 13 percent of elderly Hispanic owner-households. Similarly, 6 percent of elderly white renter-households live in moderately to severely inadequate housing, compared to 21 percent of elderly black and 16 percent of elderly Hispanic renter-households (Mikelsons and Turner, 1991). Dramatic differences also exist among different income groups: Of elderly households with incomes between $10,000 and $15,000, 4.4 percent live in moderately to severely inadequate housing compared to 8.7 percent of those with incomes between $5,000 and $10,000 and 17.4 percent of those with incomes below $5,000.

Of equal importance to the condition of housing is the availability of features that support the ability of older people to carry out tasks and activities. Most housing occupied by the elderly was built for active persons who function independently. Such dwelling units often have stairs, high thresholds between rooms, inadequate lighting, and bathing facilities that are difficult for older people to use easily and safely. Only about 6.6 percent of dwelling units occupied by elderly-headed households with health or mobility problems have such basic features as grab bars and handrails (Struyk, 1987). Almost 50 percent of severely frail elderly living alone reside in dwelling units with no special supportive features (Soldo and Longino, 1988). An estimated 20 percent of the dwelling units of the elderly are in need of modification or repair.

STRATEGIES TO INCREASE HOME MODIFICATION AND REPAIR

Strategies to increase the incidence of home modification and repair include more widespread and systematic home assessments, increased public awareness about the role of the environment, and the creation of more programs that provide affordable home modification and repair services.

Improving Assessments

An important element in creating a home environment that is safe and supportive is an assessment of its condition and suitability, but very few dwelling units are systematically assessed. Professionals who assess the environment include occupational therapists, case managers, inspectors associated with neighborhood rehabilitation programs, and energy specialists from weatherization programs.

Considerable variation exists in what is evaluated and the emphasis given to the environment. For example, staff who work for weatherization or home security programs generally concern themselves only with attributes of the dwelling unit that their agencies can change. They usually do not assess the suitability of the home in terms of its supportiveness for frail residents. On the other hand, case managers often overlook physical aspects of the environment or underestimate their importance. Consequently, physical modifications that could obviate or reduce the need for services are not part of the care plan.

Methods of assessment vary widely. Some assessments systematically evaluate features of the environment while others are open-ended, relying on the professional judgment of the assessor. Comprehensive assessments link an older person's ability to carry out activities of daily living and instrumental activities of daily living independently with an evaluation of the home's ability to provide support (Trickey, 1989). Typically, such an assessment relies on a questionnaire and a visual inspection of the home, using a checklist of areas and features. In some cases, a nurse or an occupational therapist observes how an older person carries out a particular task, thereby providing a more accurate sense of both personal capabilities and interaction with the environment. This type of assessment is especially appropriate for frail elderly and should be used more frequently. In reality, however, many homes of even very frail elderly go unassessed, and the supportive qualities of the dwelling units of the rest of the population receive scant attention. Home assessments, using a common method that includes a minimal set of home environmental features, need to be more available.

Expanding Public Awareness

Even if home assessments become more widespread and better methods are developed, realistically only a relatively few elderly will benefit directly because of the costs of assessment and a lack of appreciation of the importance of the environment. Therefore, an accompanying strategy is to raise the awareness of older people and the public about the role played by the home environment in avoiding accidents and promoting independence. This awareness can lead to increased advocacy for publicly funded home modification/repair and more interest in making "preventive" changes.

A number of programs that include slides or videos to educate older people about the home environment have been developed and could be used in group settings like senior centers and daycare centers (AARP, 1986; Creedon et al., 1989; Johns Hopkins University Injury Prevention Center, 1991). Individuals can also be encouraged to use materials developed to help them in (1) assessing their own home environments; (2) solving problems (e.g., how to tack down a throw rug or lower a threshold); (3) obtaining products; and (4) locating providers who can make changes (Branson, 1991; Ostroff, 1989; Pynoos and Cohen, 1990; Pynoos, Cohen and Lucas, 1988).

Most educational programs focus on safety, but many older people do not alter their environment until an accident has occurred or until they can no longer perform tasks because of chronic health problems. Peer group discussions, in which participants talk about accidents they have had and ways to avoid them, may heighten awareness. Resource centers that include displays of homelike and attractive ways to modify homes may also raise awareness. Rather than focusing only on safety, it may be better to emphasize how alterations can also make life easier and the home more comfortable.

Developing Home Modification and Repair Programs

There is an adage to the effect that we do a disservice to clients if they are "all assessed with nowhere to go." A predominant problem has been the lack of providers who have the trust of older clients and the skills to make home modification and repairs.

Home repairs are often done by residents themselves as evidenced by the "do it yourself" movement, but many older women (whose gender roles did not encompass making repairs) and frail elderly may not have the experience or ability to make alterations. This is especially true if the changes are complicated, numerous, and require special skills, strength, or tools—as in constructing a ramp. Even apparently simple changes can be complicated. For example, grab bars should be attached to studs in the wall and installed at the correct angle and height in relation to the person using them. Hence, it may be necessary to employ a provider such as a remodeler, a handyman, a medical supply company, or an agency to make changes. Remodelers have generally preferred larger jobs such as complete kitchens or bathrooms, and medical supply companies have focused on installing hardware items that they sell. Older people are often concerned about the reliability, skills, and honesty of such private sector providers.

Over the past decade, hundreds of nonprofit programs have been created to make home modifications and repairs. While the total number of agencies providing such services is unknown, a recent survey has catalogued at least 300 programs (Long Term Care National Resource Center, 1991). The programs tend to be small and serve, on average, about 240 clients per year with an annual budget of $268,000. Budgets range from zero for programs using donated labor and materials to several million dollars for programs involved in major rehabilitation or weatherization. On the average, about half of all program budgets are spent on repairs, with the remaining money split fairly evenly among modifications, safety/security, and upkeep/weatherization services. Most of these programs are part of larger organizations, such as community action and weatherization agencies, and city and county governments.

Programs that carry out home modification and repairs must deal with a variety of service delivery tasks like ordering and storing materials, dealing with specialized trades and unions, securing tools, estimating costs, licensing, subcontracting, and managing liability and quality control. These tasks can prove challenging and difficult for agencies like visiting nurses associations, whose work has primarily involved providing professional human services.

Programs deliver modification and repair services using a variety of models. Some carry out all the work using their own staff in order to ensure accountability and responsiveness. Other programs employ some staff —supervisors/assessors and handymen, for example—to carry out routine, smaller jobs but subcontract work requiring licensed tradespeople such as electricians and plumbers. An increasing number of programs use volunteers. In addition, some programs train older people to make their own modifications and supply them with tools. More comprehensive programs combine models of service delivery so that they can provide more service in a timely and cost-effective manner.

INCREASING FINANCIAL SUPPORT TO PAY
FOR REPAIRS AND MODIFICATIONS

While many alterations are low cost, others are too expensive for persons with low incomes—those who need them most. There are several sources to help the elderly pay for alterations to their homes. With a prescription from a doctor, Medicare and Medicaid will pay for some approved assistive devices related to recovery from acute health incidents (e.g., a hip fracture). These devices are generally medically-oriented hardware items such as hospital beds, walkers, and raised toilet seats. Other programs, such as Community Development and Social Service Block Grants, the Farmer's Home Administration, and the Older Americans Act, have been tapped to provide funds for ramps, security (e.g., new locks), and a variety of general repairs. These programs operate on a loan, sliding fee, or grant basis. Some programs provide free labor if the client pays for materials.

Programs have very limited budgets and are often restricted by their funding sources in the number of clients they can serve and in the types of alterations they can make. Many programs serve only one or two communities or even small neighborhoods, leaving many areas uncovered. Therefore, many older people have to use their own money to pay for alterations, a disincentive if the changes are costly, income is low, and functional status is such that they will have to move in a short period of time.

Because there is no national home modification and repair program, as noted above, agencies turn to a variety of sources for funds and must compete with many other needs. According to a recent survey of home modification and repair programs (Pynoos et al., in press), the two most frequently cited funding sources are Older Americans Act Title III and Title V funds (39 percent) and block grants (38 percent). Title III and Title V, however, contribute only 5 percent of total program budgets whereas block grants contribute 39 percent. Block grants are generally oriented toward housing rehabilitation in specific neighborhoods, leaving other less-well-funded programs such as Title III to pay for smaller repairs and modifications.

Neither the appropriations for the Older Americans Act nor Community Development Block Grants have grown much over the last five years. Programs, therefore, also rely on cities, counties, and states, and on foundations and charitable contributions. Of these sources, only state funds contributed a substantial proportion (16 percent) of overall budgets. Thirty-two percent of programs reported receiving client payments, which contributed only an average of 5 percent to program budgets—understandable given that most programs serve low- and moderate-income persons.

State-supported home modification and repair programs seem to be on the increase, although how they will fare in a recessionary period is yet to be seen. In 1990, Ohio allocated $4.1 million to create and expand innovative housing options, including home repair and modification. In that same year, Maryland awarded grants to local organizations, including area agencies on aging (AAAs), to provide minor repairs and maintenance of properties occupied by low-income elderly and hand-icapped individuals. Similarly, the Rhode Island Housing Mortgage Finance Corporation and the Minnesota Home Finance Agency have provided low-interest loans for home repairs and improvements. Maine voters approved a bond issue in 1989 that established a state-funded low-interest loan program for adaptive equipment.

PROMOTING UNIVERSAL HOUSING

Many problems that existing home environments present for aging in place would be eliminated if supportive, adaptable, and accessible housing were built in the first place, the goal of a worldwide movement toward universal housing. A *universal house* would include features such as wheelchair-accessible entryways, kitchens, and bathrooms; single lever faucets; nonslip flooring; easy to reach temperature controls; antiscald devices; and grab bars. The principles of universal housing are encapsulated in the Fair Housing Act of 1988, which requires that buildings containing over four units provide basic accessibility and provisions for adding features like grab bars. New construction, however, adds only about 2 percent to the housing stock each year, and the act exempts smaller buildings and single family homes. Hence, efforts are still needed to make the existing stock more suitable for frail older and disabled younger persons.

CREATING A NATIONAL HOME-MODIFICATION PROGRAM

The current system for making the existing housing stock suitable for older people is fragmented, uncoordinated, inadequately funded, and full of gaps in coverage. Most of the funds are spent on repairs and energy conservation. Consequently, the homes of many frail elderly go unassessed and unmodified. Strategies such as improving assessments, expanding public awareness, and enhancing programs could help increase the incidence of home modification and repair. In addition, expanding Medicare and Medicaid coverage to include more types of assistive devices and modifications would help.

Home repair and modification agencies could also attempt to gain more resources through Housing and Urban Development (HUD) programs that emanate from the National Affordable Housing Act (NAHA) of 1990, which places a new emphasis on supportive housing and aging in place. For example, NAHA's HOME Investment Partnership program will provide funds through formula grants and model projects to expand the supply of affordable housing with an emphasis on rental units. HOME includes a provision for home repair services for elderly and disabled homeowners, with preference given to very low income families and individuals with physical and mental disabilities.

Another opportunity for programs is active participation in the Comprehensive Housing Affordability Strategy (CHAS), a five-year planning process mandated by NAHA to establish housing priorities for state and local areas. The process of developing a CHAS requires conferring with appropriate social services agencies regarding the housing needs of the elderly.

Repair and modification would be greatly accelerated by the creation of a National Home Modification Program. It could be modeled on a HUD-funded eight-site demonstration program that occurred in the 1980s. A similar and larger experiment, "Assisted Agency Services," took place in England from 1985 to 1990 (Leather and Mackintosh, 1990). The English version involved 74 agencies, each of which received 50 percent of approximately a £200,000 budget from the national government and the rest from a variety of other sources including cities and towns. Drawing on the British and United States experience, the National Home Modification Program would focus on increasing the suitability of existing dwelling units for lower income frail elderly and younger people with disabilities. Measures of frailty and disability could be based on activities of daily living and instrumental activities of daily living. The program would provide local agencies with core public funding to carry out assessments and home modifications related to safety, accessibility, and functioning. Sponsoring agencies could include weatherization programs, nursing associations, area agencies on aging, and housing authorities. Agencies would be required to use a common, broad-based environmental and functional assessment instrument, set up a professional advisory committee, and keep data for evaluation. Even though client payments or fees would be expected to make up only a small percentage of agency budgets, they would be mandated to help ensure service choice and critical feedback. Incentives would be provided for using donated labor and materials as well as for coordinating services and benefits with other programs such as Medicare, Medicaid, and weatherization.

The passage of a National Home Modification program would face a number of obstacles related to the federal budget. It would become a reality only if it had widespread support from the aging and disabled communities. For such support to exist, home modification and repair need to be seen by professionals, older people, and public officials as a key factor in supporting aging in place.

* * *

Jon Pynoos, Ph.D., is UPS Foundation Associate Professor of Gerontology and director, National Eldercare Institute on Housing and Supportive, services, Andrus Gerontology Center, University of Southern California, Los Angeles.

REFERENCES

AARP, 1986. *Falls and Fires: Safety in the Home* [Slides and audiocassette]. Washington, D.C.: American Association of Retired Persons.

Branson, G., 1991. *The Complete Guide to Barrier-free Housing: Convenient Living for the Elderly and the Physically Handicapped.* White Hall, Va.: Betterway Publications.

Creedon, M. A. et al., 1989. "Home Safety." *Project Independence* [Slides, slide narrative, and audiocassette]. Washington, D.C.: National Council on the Aging.

Johns Hopkins University Injury Prevention Center, 1991. *Home Safe Home* [Videocassette]. Baltimore, Md.: Johns Hopkins.

Lawton, M. P., 1980. "Housing the Elderly, Residential Quality and Residential Satisfaction." *Research on Aging* 2: 309–28.

Leather, P. and Mackintosh, S., 1990. *Monitoring Assisted Agency Services: Home Improvement Agencies—An Evaluation of Performance.* London: HMSO Publications Centre.

Long Term Care National Resource Center at UCLA/USC, 1991. *National Directory of Home Modification and Repair Programs.* Los Angeles: Long Term Care National Resource Center at UCLA/USC.

Mikelsons, M. and Turner, M., 1991. *Housing Conditions of the Elderly in the 1980s: A Data Book.* Washington, D.C.: Urban Institute.

Ostroff, E., 1989. *A Consumer's Guide to Home Adaptation.* (Available from The Adaptive Environments Center, 374 Congress St., Suite 301, Boston, MA 02210.)

Pynoos, J., 1988. *Home Modification for Frail Older Persons:Policy Barriers and New Directions.* Paper presented at the meeting of the National Conference on Low-Income Older Homeowners, sponsored by American Association of Retired Persons.

Pynoos, J., in press. "Home Modification and Repair." In A. Monk, ed., *Columbia Handbook on Retirement.* New York: Columbia University Press.

Pynoos, J. and Cohen, E., 1990. *Home Safety Guide for Older People: Check It Out / Fix It Up.* Washington, D.C.: Serif Press.

Pynoos, J., Cohen, E. and Lucas, C., 1988. *The Caring Home Booklet: Environmental Coping Strategies for Alzheimer's Caregivers.* Los Angeles: Long Term Care National Resource Center at UCLA/USC.

Pynoos, J. et al., 1987. "Home Modifications: Improvements That Extend Independence." In V. Regnier and J. Pynoos, eds., *Housing the Aged: Design Directives and Policy Considerations.* New York: Elsevier Science Publishing Co., pp. 277–303.

Pynoos, J. et al., in press. *Home Modification Guidebook.* Los Angeles: Long Term Care National Resource Center at UCLA/USC.

Soldo, B. and Longino, C., 1988. "Social and Physical Environment for the Vulnerable Aged." In *America's Aging: The Social and Built Environment.* Institute of Medicine and National Research Council. Washington, D.C.: National Academy Press, pp. 103–33.

Struyk, R., 1987. "Housing Adaptations: Needs and Practices." In V. Regnier and J. Pynoos, eds., *Housing the Aged: Design Directives and Policy Considerations.* New York: Elsevier Science Publishing Co., pp. 259–75.

Trickey, F., 1989. *Maintaining Seniors' Independence: A Guide to Home Adaptations.* Montreal: Public Affairs Centre CMHC.

Chapter 5

Aging in Place: The Role of Families

Barbara M. Silverstone and Amy Horowitz

"Aging in place" is a relatively new term that has been used to describe the phenomenon of growing older within a specific environmental setting. While early definitions of aging in place focused on older persons' preference to grow old in their own home, more recent work has expanded the scope as well as the conceptual complexity of the term. Both Lawton (1990) and Pynoos (1990), for example, have stressed the dynamic nature of aging in place, in that both the individual and the environment are in process of change over time. Both also emphasize, as a result, the importance of continuously reassessing the person-environment fit. These perspectives, which capture the dynamic nature of aging in place, are especially relevant in assessing the role of families in this process, as they both influence and are influenced by this phenomenon over time.

Given the extent to which family relations have dominated the gerontological literature over the past several decades, it is somewhat surprising that the literature on aging in place contains relatively few direct references to family behaviors or attitudes as contributory factors that may either promote or hinder an older person's ability to age in place. Still fewer studies exist on the impact such decisions may have on the families themselves. There is little question, however, that aging in place, or moving elsewhere, is heavily influenced by family considerations. It can be assumed that most families play some role, for better or worse, in the decision of where to live, particularly when there is concern about the real or potential frailty of the older relative. This role, however, tends to be assumed rather than explored in the current research literature.

The purpose of this chapter is to explicitly examine the role of families in influencing the dynamic processes of aging in place. Three broad areas can be identified to organize this discussion: (1) family considerations in late-life migration patterns, (2) family caregiving behavior and consequences, and (3) personal autonomy negotiations within a family context. We will briefly review the research evidence in the first two areas, while focusing most of our discussion on the relevance of personal autonomy considerations to both understanding and enhancing the family decision-making processes surrounding aging in place.

FAMILY CONSIDERATIONS IN LATE-LIFE MIGRATION PATTERNS

Research focusing on migration trends consistently finds that the elderly are much less likely to relocate than are younger persons (e.g., Myers, 1982). Yet, when making comparisons between those older people who choose to remain in place and those who choose to move, one needs to take into account the types of moves this population makes. Using data from the 1983 Annual Housing Survey, Speare and Meyer (1988) identified two categories of mobility. The first category includes those who move for amenity or retirement reasons, and the second consists of those who move because of widowhood or kinship proximity. Similarly, Serow (1988), in his study of cross-national comparisons of elderly moves, found that the two life-cycle events most likely to trigger migration in later life are retirement and widowhood. Those who moved for retirement or amenity reasons were the younger and relatively more affluent elderly. Among the older elderly, moves were more likely to be based on the need for care and support.

A developmental perspective of elderly migration was taken by Litwak and Longino (1987), who describe three types of moves: retirement moves; moves due to moderate disability; and, finally, moves due to major chronic disability resulting in institutional care. "Social pressure for three basic moves derives from the ability of older people in the first stage of their retirement to live at some distance from their children and their need at the second and third states for their children, or a combination of children and institution to help them (p. 267)."

Thus, the literature on migration in later life clearly highlights the importance of family considerations in motivating relocation decisions, especially at later life stages. As need for care and support increases, the desire or necessity for kinship proximity represents a significant incentive to move closer to (or back to) areas where family, especially children, are located.

FAMILY CAREGIVING BEHAVIOR AND STRESSES

Although it is not our intention to review the vast research literature compiled on family caregiving, we would be remiss in not calling attention to the relevance of this body of knowledge to understanding how families both influence and are influenced by the elder's decisions regarding aging in place.

Research has consistently documented that families are the primary providers of long-term-care services to the frail and disabled elderly living in the community (see, for example, Horowitz, 1985; Stone, Cafferata and Sangl, 1987). Three-fourths of community-dwelling frail elders receive all their support from family and friends (Scanlon, 1988). Based on data from the 1982 National Long Term Care Survey, Newman (1990) has estimated that approximately four times as many frail elderly live in residential settings as live in nursing homes. There is no doubt that most of the people in the former group are aging in place primarily because of the emotional, financial, instrumental, and personal care services that families provide to support them in their residential setting.

Although seldom explored in depth, the importance of family support as a contributing factor to aging in place has been recognized by several writers in the field. Chevan (1987), for example, notes that "having a spouse or child to help in maintaining a home may be as essential as having necessary economic resources (p. 232)." Tilson and Fahey (1990) include the presence of family/spouse to provide help with activities of daily life as one of three factors, along with sufficient income and availability of community services, that influence the ability of the elderly to continue living in their own homes. The specific role of informal supports to the elderly aging in the community was examined in a longitudinal study of aging in place, and it was found that informal care was the norm, with almost three-quarters of the elderly receiving some assistance from family or friends (Morris et al., 1990). Family support has also been found to promote aging in place of tenants in senior housing: Frail tenants with supportive services provided by family or community agencies were frequently allowed to remain in their apartment units, while those without such support were often required to move out (Sheehan and Wisensale, 1991).

What the aging in place literature seldom addresses is the consequences to families of providing this support. The family caregiving literature, however, clearly indicates that this support is not without cost to the family caregivers. Negative mental health effects of caregiving have been documented across studies (see, for example, George and Gwyther, 1986; Horowitz, 1985; Pruchno and Potashnik, 1989) and apply not only to primary and proximate caregivers, but to secondary caregivers (Brody et al., 1989) and geographically distant caregivers (Schoonover et al., 1988) as well. Furthermore, a fairly consistent finding across studies is that the emotional stresses associated with caregiving are the most pervasive and the most difficult for the caregiver to deal with when compared to either the physical or financial aspects of care. For most caregivers, these emotional strains stem from a constant concern for the older person's health and safety (Horowitz, 1985), concerns that can be heightened when the elder lives alone in a residential environment that is concurrently aging and potentially dangerous.

Thus, it is clear that aging in place does not, and cannot, take place in a vacuum, especially when disability or frailty is involved. Rather, it is a process that takes place within a family context. Whether or not an elder desires or is able to age in place is often a function of the availability and willingness of family members to provide needed support; this support, in turn, will have inevitable consequences, both negative and positive, for the entire family system.

PERSONAL AUTONOMY AND
FAMILY DECISION-MAKING

While research on migration and family-care patterns provides a macro-level picture of the role families play in facilitating the phenomenon of aging in place, conceptual issues relevant to autonomy in later life can better illuminate the complex considerations and processes by which a decision is reached and then continuously reevaluated by the elderly and their family members.

The personal autonomy of older people is clearly exercised in their decision to age in place, not only as an expression of a preferred lifestyle but as a means of further enhancing their autonomy. Tilson and Fahey (1990), for example, have described a house as a manifestation of one's power to choose and exercise autonomy. Old people have been found to feel more in control of their lives living in familiar surroundings, even in situations that are objectively detrimental to the quality of their lives. The psychological benefits of retaining autonomy apparently outweigh other considerations.

Concern has been raised about the potential of family members for compromising the personal autonomy of older persons by actively encouraging, and sometimes insisting on, a move to a "safer" environment. However, short of those situations involving physical coercion or legal action, the actual identification of family transactions that result in a loss of personal autonomy for the older person is far from easy. The subtlety and complexity of family relationships confound any singular characterization. Furthermore, preliminary research findings (Horowitz, Silverstone and Reinhardt, 1991) suggest that family members are extremely sensitive to the autonomy needs of their older relatives, often more so than are the elders themselves. Whereas families recognized and gave priority to the elder's exercise of autonomy, elders more often gave greater weight to ensuring personal health and safety than to maintaining personal control (Horowitz, Silverstone and Reinhardt, 1991). Lawton (1985) cautions that we must look at residential status as being determined by a series of decisions, the most frequent of which is to remain in place, that are primarily made by the older person. According to Lawton, "the number of instances where the decision is out of the person's hands because of public or private actions of others, or because of family decision making, is very small (p. 45)." Thus, the family's role in the decision-making process regarding aging in place is more appropriately characterized as one of participant rather than as adversary.

A clear understanding, therefore, is required of what is meant by personal autonomy. Definitions such as "independence" and "self-determination" do not suffice when attempts are made to unravel family transactions around issues like "aging in place." The components of personal autonomy must be determined and then applied to practical everyday situations.

One approach to conceptualization defines personal autonomy as the "exercise of self-determined, goal-oriented behavior that is or can be otentially threatened or inhibited (or supported and encouraged) by a variety of circumstances, real or symbolic, intrinsic or external to the person (Silverstone, 1987). Emphasized in this formulation is the importance of evaluating autonomy within the context of an individual's idiosyncratic goals. Credence has been given to this approach in a recent study of visually impaired older persons and their families (Horowitz, Silverstone and Reinhardt, 1991) and its applicability appears useful in attempting to analyze family situations related to the phenomenon of aging in place.

The goals of a particular older person must first be clearly understood. To simply say that the goal is to "grow old in one's own home" provides little useful information for two primary reasons.

First, this global goal statement masks the specific components of aging in place that are of particular importance to that older person. One person's desire to remain in place may, in fact, reflect a psychological attachment to the specific housing unit, that is, the home as the repository for family memories or as a familiar setting that confers an increasingly rare feeling of competence. For another person, the same articulated goal may more accurately reflect an attachment to specific furnishings or the status of homeowner. For still another elder, it is the attachment to neighborhood, community, and established friendships that primarily drives the desire to age in place. Each underlying goal suggests different options as well as priorities for action on the part of the elderly and their families when faced with a deteriorating housing situation or increasing frailty of the elder. For example, where the primary attachment is to the specific residence, one would focus on environmental modifications or infusion of in-home supportive services. In contrast, where the attachment to community is primary, options for more appropriate housing within the same geographic area can be pursued to meet the primary goal of the elder.

The second reason global goal statements are limited is that persons of any age seldom have single overriding goals. Rather, for any one individual, goals can be multiple, contradictory, long or short range, and have different priorities. Two important, but seemingly contradictory goals of the elder—to remain in his or her home and to be in a safe environment—can coexist at any one time and can shift in priority over time with changes in the health status of the elder, the residential environment, and the family resources available to support the elder. As frailty and disability become a reality, the goal of aging in place may recede in importance for the elder compared to goals related to maintaining his or her own or family's emotional and physical well-being.

For example, adult children may be strongly committed to providing support and help to aging parents but also have other concurrent goals related to their careers or to the care of other family members. The worry and anxiety caused by an aging parent living in an unsafe environment may interfere with these other goals. Family members who eschew these other considerations in their lives and pretend that the welfare of the older person is their only concern make it difficult for older persons to deal with and reassess, if needed, their own situation. It is important to note that an implicit goal of many older people is to contribute to the well-being of the entire family unit by, at the very least, "doing no harm."

What is the role of the family in these diverse but real scenarios? How can they carry out their filial responsibilities without impeding the elder's self-directed goal-determined behavior? In such situations family members do best by working with the elder relative to articulate their multiple concurrent goals, as well as to clarify for themselves and the elder the family's goals. A meaningful dialogue, with both parties placing their goals on the table, can, through compromise and negotiation, lead to imaginative and workable plans.

The primary threat to personal autonomy in these situations comes into play when unrealistic promises are made to fulfill goals for the elder or the family. A case in point is the situation where older relatives are persuaded to leave their lifelong homes and communities to be nearer sons or daughters who give assurances that their new lives will be socially rich—only to find that they are isolated from age peers and familiar pursuits. Family members are better off to assess in advance their ability to substitute for the myriad social contacts that have been built up by older people who have lived for many years in one place. The same point can be made for elders who are persuaded, often against their initial reservations, to maintain the "family home," when, in fact, relocating to a more socially rich environment would have been more in line with the elder's primary goals.

In the vast majority of cases, however, it is important to remember that the primary impediment to aging in place is neither family over-protectiveness nor lack of concern. Rather, barriers to the exercise of personal autonomy in decision making over where to live are primarily obstacles in the physical environment as well as the older person's changing mental or physical condition. These are common enemies that older people and their family members can confront together. Finally, family members do well to keep in mind that their interactions with aging relatives over where to live can be, for the most part, an enormously helpful process and, given the dynamic nature of aging in place, one that continues over time.

ACKNOWLEDGMENT

The authors would like to acknowledge the contribution of Robin McInerney, M.A., in preparing this chapter.

* * *

Barbara M. Silverstone, D.S.W., is executive director, and Amy Horowitz, D.S.W., is director of research and evaluation, both at The Lighthouse, Inc., New York.

REFERENCES

Brody, E. M. et al., 1989. "Caregiving Daughters and Their Local Siblings: Perceptions, Strain, and Interactions." *Gerontologist,* 29: 529–38.

Chevan, A., 1987. "Homeownership in the Older Population." *Research on Aging,* 9: 226–55.

George, L. K. and Gwyther, L. P., 1986. "Caregiver Well-Being: A Multidimensional Examination of Family Caregivers of Demented Adults." *Gerontologist* 26: 253–59.

Horowitz, A., 1985. "Family Caregiving to the Frail Elderly." In M. P. Lawton and G. L. Maddox, eds., *Annual Review of Gerontology and Geriatrics* 5: 194–246.

Horowitz, A., Silverstone, B. M. and Reinhardt, J., 1991. "A Conceptual and Empirical Exploration of Personal Autonomy Issues Within Family Caregiving Relationships." *Gerontologist* 31: 23–31.

Lawton, M. P., 1985. "Housing and Living Environments of Older People." In R. H. Binstock and E. Shanas, eds., *The Handbook of Aging and the Social Sciences,* 2d ed. New York:Van Nostrand Reinhold, pp. 450–57.

Lawton, M. P., 1990. "Knowledge Resources and Gaps in Housing for the Aged." In D. Tilson, ed., *Aging in Place: Supporting the Frail Elderly in Residential Environments.* Glenview, Ill.: Scott, Foresman.

Litwak, E. and Longino, C. F., 1987. "Migration Patterns Among the Elderly: A Developmental Perspective." *Gerontologist,* 27(3): 266–72.

Morris, J. N. et al., 1990. "Aging in Place: A Longitudinal Example." In D. Tilson, ed., *Aging in Place: Supporting the Frail Elderly in Residential Environments.* Glenview, Ill.: Scott, Foresman.

Myers, P., 1982. *Aging in Place: Strategies to Help the Elderly Stay in Revitalizing Neighborhoods.* Washington, D.C.: Conservation Foundation.

Newman, S., 1990. "The Frail Elderly in the Community: An Overview of Characteristics." In D. Tilson, ed., *Aging in Place: Supporting the Frail Elderly in Residential Environments.* Glenview, Ill.: Scott, Foresman.

Pruchno, R. A. and Potashnik, S. L., 1989. "Caregiving Spouses: Physical and Mental Perspectives." *Journal of the American Geriatrics Society* 37: 697–705.

Pynoos, J., 1990. "Public Policy and Aging in Place: Identifying the Problems and Potential Solutions." In D. Tilson, ed., *Aging in Place: Supporting the Frail Elderly in Residential Environments*. Glenview, Ill.: Scott, Foresman.

Scanlon, W. J., 1988. "A Perspective on Long-Term Care for the Elderly." *Health Care Financing Review, Annual Supplement:* 7–15.

Schoonover, C. B. et al., 1988. "Parent Care and Geographically Distant Children." *Research on Aging* 10: 472–92.

Serow, W. J., 1988. "Why the Elderly Move." *Research on Aging* 9: 582–97.

Sheehan, N. W. and Wisensale, S. K., 1991. "'Aging in Place': Discharge Policies and Procedures Concerning Frailty Among Senior Housing Tenants." *Journal of Gerontological Social Work* 16: 109–23.

Silverstone, B. M., 1987. "Enhancing Personal Autonomy for Frail Elderly and Disabled Persons." Arthur and Katherine Sehlin Lecture, University of Minnesota, Minneapolis.

Speare, A. and Meyer, J. W., 1988. "Types of Elderly Residential Mobility and Their Determinants." *Journal of Gerontology, Social Sciences* 43: S74–81.

Stone, R., Cafferata, G. L. and Sangl, J., 1987. "Caregivers of the Frail Elderly: A National Profile." *Gerontologist* 27: 616–26.

Tilson, D. and Fahey, C., 1990. "Introduction." In D. T. Tilson, ed., *Aging in Place: Supporting the Frail Elderly in Residential Environments*. Glenview, Ill.: Scott, Foresman.

Chapter 6

If You Build It, They May Not Come

Leah Dobkin

The senior housing industry, continuing care retirement communities, and congregate developments reached a feverish pitch of expansion in the early and mid 1980s. The traditional nonprofit, religious-affiliated housing sponsor no longer dominated the field. Other nonprofit organizations and for-profit companies joined the ranks. Many say too fast. "There's gold in the silver market" was the battle cry. Most developers were targeting the healthier and wealthier elders.

Many housing products were tested to entice older people out of their homes. Continuing care retirement communities began to unbundle service packages and offer long-term-care health insurance products linked to their communities. Congregate housing offered a new elegance in the form of flowered, pastel-colored rooms. Some older people flocked to these facilities, but generally they were older, more frail and smaller in numbers than the senior housing industry had anticipated.

Vacancy rates exceeded projected goals, resulting in marketing budgets soaring to between $5,000 and $7,000 per resident. Some facilities experienced serious financial troubles and consequently raised their fees, lowered their services, or sold their projects.

One survival strategy aimed at fixing distressed projects was to convert congregate housing into assisted living. That is, housing facilities that provided meals, transportation, housekeeping, and social activities upgraded their service package to include personal care, such as assistance with bathing and dressing, and 24-hour supervision or some other degree of protective oversight. The theory was that the older, frailer segment of the market is more highly motivated to avoid a nursing home and less likely to be able to afford or manage extensive services in their current home. As a result, "rent up" periods (the phase after building the project when the owner begins to market the facility to renters) would be shorter and vacancy rates lower than in simple congregate housing. The latter part of the 1980s and early 1990s have witnessed an expansion of converted and new assisted living facilities. In fact, rent-up periods have generally been shorter, but turnover of residents has been greater than in congregate housing, and turnover costs owners money.

With the exception of this segment of the industry, new senior housing production has slowed up considerably. Developers complain that lenders will not lend, and lenders complain that projects are too risky.

WHAT HAPPENED?

Developers say that older consumers are misinformed about retirement communities and just do not understand the product. Housing activists say that what is being built is the wrong product and not what consumers want or can afford. There is truth in both statements, but there is another major factor: The preference of older people to "age in place" is strong and growing.

The American Association of Retired Persons conducts a national housing survey every three years to identify consumer preferences, concerns, and needs. The survey also tracks emerging housing changes and trends. The latest survey showed that 86 percent of older people wish to stay in their homes and never move (AARP, 1990). This number increased from 78 percent in 1986 (AARP, 1986). Older people who most want to stay in their current homes include those over 75, those with annual incomes of less than $12,000 a year, widowed people, and those living in naturally occurring retirement communities—buildings or neighborhoods in which the majority of residents are at least 60 years of age (AARP, 1990). These same subgroups are also most likely to live alone and to prefer to live alone. Many do not have the resources to move to what might be more appropriate housing options, and they lack a support system that could provide or manage critical home-delivered services. Determining how to creatively and affordably maintain these people in their homes of choice will be the greatest challenge to public policy makers and to housing, health, and social service providers.

The AARP findings were also supported by the 1980 and 1987 American Housing Surveys (which are compared in an Urban Institute Report soon to be published by AARP). The percentage of older households living at their present address for 20 years or more increased from 50.6 in 1980 to 60.7 in 1987, and only 30 percent of older renters reported moving in the last three years, compared to 71 percent of renters under age 65 (Turner and Mickelsons, 1992).

Another national survey (Princeton Survey Research Associates, 1991) found that the older people most likely to think they will always live in their home are over 70 years of age and live alone (78 percent), are limited functionally (72 percent), and have an income below $25,000 (77 percent). The subgroup most expecting to age in place were homeowners who had income less than $6,000 a year (87 percent) (AARP, 1990).

TO MOVE OR NOT TO MOVE

Do older people truly prefer to remain in their homes, or do they really prefer to move but have barriers that prevent that action? Barriers include being unable to sell a home in a soft real estate market and also limited resources and energy. Barriers can also include a shortage of affordable and attractive alternatives, as mentioned earlier. There are a variety of push-and-pull factors that influence an older consumer's decision to move or stay put. AARP's (1990) housing survey revealed that older people's main housing concerns were indoor and outdoor maintenance and the rising cost of utilities and property taxes. These can be push factors, but more affordable and reliable home and outdoor maintenance services and home repair and modification programs can tip the decision-making scale toward aging in place. So can property tax relief and energy efficiency programs. There are also promising indicators that housing alternatives such as reverse mortgages, shared housing, elder cottages, and accessory apartments are helping people to age in place by providing increased income, reduced expenses, and opportunities to barter shelter for needed services.

Factors tipping the scale toward moving could include specialized packing and moving services for elders that reduce the anxiety of moving; more low, moderate, middle, and mixed income facilities; facilities that offer indoor and outdoor maintenance services; and health promotion and personal care services. Consumers who are interested in moving generally prefer to remain in their own city and county or small towns and suburbs elsewhere (AARP, 1990). More older people would be tempted to move if facilities were built where older people currently live and in these small towns and suburbs.

LACK OF PLANNING

There is an unresolved debate as to whether aging in place is a "nondecision." AARP's (1990) housing survey supports the premise that it is. Over half of older people have done very little or no planning for their future housing needs, and 88 percent have not consulted with anyone about their housing (AARP, 1990). The subgroups that have done no planning are also the most vulnerable. They are people over 75, those with incomes of less than $12,000 per year, widowed people, people who are divorced, separated or never married, renters, and those with a number of health limitations. Expectations to age in place may be unrealistic for these nonplanners.

Why do older Americans not plan? Because they are Americans! Our dominant culture is obsessed with the here and now. Yet reality dictates that as we age most of us will need to plan our housing before a crisis if we are intent on preserving our home of choice. We will need to make some housing adjustment. We will either move or modify our current housing situation to better suit our needs. A housing decision will have to be made, but who will make it? Twenty-two percent of older people expect to move, but only 13 percent would like to move (AARP, 1990). This suggests that almost one out of ten older people expect to move against their wishes. Poor planning may force older people out of their homes.

CONCLUSION

A functional assessment tool for older people and their families (which will be available through AARP in the summer of 1992) is now being developed to help them plan ahead and evaluate the convenience, comfort, and safety of their homes. Such a tool, coupled with local educational efforts to help midlife and older people evaluate their current and future housing needs and options, is invaluable. It takes more than the magic of movies to ensure that if you build it, they will come. It takes better-conceived projects that offer the price, services, and location older consumers want as well as need. It also takes an increased effort to help consumers make more informed decisions about their housing. Then if you build it, they may very well come. And if they come, their adjustment and tenure can be greatly improved.

*   *   *

Leah Dobkin, M.S., is a senior program specialist for consumer affairs, American Association of Retired Persons, Washington, D.C.

REFERENCES

AARP, 1986. "Understanding Senior Housing: An American Association of Retired Persons Survey of Consumer Preferences, Concerns and Needs." Washington, D.C.

AARP, 1990. "Understanding Senior Housing for the 1990's. An American Association of Retired Persons Survey of Consumer Preferences, Concerns and Needs." Washington, D.C.

Princeton Survey Research Associates, 1991. "AARP's 12th Annual Survey of Middle Aged and Older Americans." Washington, D.C. Unpublished report to AARP.

Turner, M. and Mickelsons, M., 1992. "Unpublished Urban Institute Chart book on Elderly Housing." Washington, D.C.: AARP.

Chapter 7

The Hartford House:
Home Modifications in Action

Beverly Hynes-Grace

Seeing may be believing, but touching is sometimes even more convincing. Visitors to The Hartford House see and touch doors and faucets with easily operated handles, thermostats and telephones with large numbers, table lamps that turn on and off with just a touch rather than a twist, a nonscalding hot water device, fire-retardant furnishings, a stove that reduces risk of clothing fire.

On display are these and a hundred more home modifications aimed at helping older people stay home, stay independent, and keep on doing the everyday things that were once so easy but now are harder because of inevitable changes in vision, hearing, mobility, agility, strength, endurance, and dexterity.

The Hartford House is an exhibit that is a real house—or at least part of a house. It comprises a full-scale living/dining room, kitchen, bedroom, bath, hall, and stairway. Throughout are modifications employing products that any person can buy, most of which do not need to be installed by a professional. The house also incorporates a variety of architectural and interior design features, such as doorways without sills (no tripping), extra lighting (improved visibility), and an absence of low coffee tables (no falling).

Unveiled in 1987, The Hartford House was a project of ITT Hartford Insurance Group, developed in cooperation with the American Association of Retired Persons (AARP). ITT Hartford, which has provided homeowners' and automobile insurance to AARP members since 1984, is one of the few U.S. firms with a corporate gerontology department.

The house was exhibited at an AARP convention in Detroit in 1988. It has also been seen in Anaheim, Atlanta, Chicago, Hartford, Houston, and New York City. Thousands of people have walked through it. Millions more can see it on a half-hour videotape and read about it in a 90-page pamphlet, both of which are free.

"The purpose of the Hartford House," according to Joan Pease, president of Partners in Planning, an Alexandria, Virginia, design firm specializing in living environments for older adults, "is to demonstrate new design concepts, helpful products, and innovative technology that can help us live longer in our homes with greater safety, security, comfort and convenience." Pease was a member of the team that developed the house.

RESOLVING A DILEMMA

Statistics only too familiar to gerontologists and others in the aging field summarize the dilemma that drove The Hartford House planning decisions. An AARP housing study (1990) found that about half of people age 60 or older had lived in their present homes for more than 20 years. Nearly 86 percent of people 60 or older—up from 78 percent in 1986—want to stay in their present home and never move.

Yet this yearning can cause concern. "Accidents are the leading cause of death among the older population," said Katrinka Smith Sloan, AARP manager of consumer affairs. "Even though younger people suffer accidents more frequently, among the older population accidents more often result in fatalities. Very often, it's an accident that will cause older persons to have to move to a nursing home because they are less mobile and unable to cope with their living environment."

We all know about this dilemma. The Hartford House includes more than 100 specific products and design features that older people—and their families—can employ to help resolve it. Perhaps a useful way to provide an overview is to cite a few examples in each of the categories cited by Pease: safety, security, comfort and convenience.

Safety

"I am very impressed with the design of The Hartford House, particularly its sensitivity to safety issues," AARP's Sloan commented.

Safety features abound in the house. For example, under the bathroom sink is a temperature control valve that prevents scalding hot water from reaching the faucets. The stove controls are at the front of the stove—no more reaching across a hot burner and a setting a sleeve afire. The stovetop burners are staggered for the same safety reason.

Grab bars on the tub/shower walls and the edge of the tub offer stability and help prevent falls. Falls on the stairway are less likely because the railings—which are installed on both sides—extend beyond the last step. Neither are there any area rugs in the house with edges to catch heels; all carpeting is wall to wall, and of dense, level-loop construction, not shag or deep pile. The carpets, upholstery, bedspreads, and all other fabrics are file-retardant. Flooring in the bathroom is rubber, which is less slippery than tile when wet.

Security

The Hartford House displays a variety of security products. Mounted on the bedroom wall is a smoke penetrating flashlight triggered by the sound of a smoke detector alarm. One touch of a special button worn on the wrist or around one's neck signals a 24-hour emergency response center to send help. Hung on the inside handle of the exterior door is a portable unit that warns against intruders by sounding an alarm when someone tries to open the door.

A portable security intercom allows identification of visitors from anywhere in the house—a feature particularly helpful to people with mobility limitations.

Comfort and Convenience

To enhance comfort and convenient living, the house employs various useful techniques. Colors of the upholstered chairs and couch in the living room contrast strongly with the flooring color, making the seat location easier for aging eyes to spot. Differentiation is also achieved through light-switch cover plates whose color is in strong contrast to that of the wall. The problem of tiny table-lamp switches that are hard to grasp is overcome by the use of lamps that turn on and off at the mere touch of a finger on the base or column.

Living room furniture includes two upholstered chairs that are close together and face each other, so that eyes can supplement ears for conversation.

Finely perforated window shades reduce glare while admitting light. Shades on lamps and the dining room chandelier also reduce glare, while focusing light on the task being illuminated. Large numerals are used on the thermostat and telephone, the oven temperature dial, the bedroom alarm clock, and the bathroom scale. Other large-print items include cookbooks, calculator, measuring tape, deck of cards, and a crossword puzzle book.

In the bathroom, a hand-held shower head supplements the conventional fixed head on the wall for seated or standing showers. In the kitchen, pot handles are angled to increase lifting leverage. Cabinet door handles are large and easy to grasp, and overhead cabinets are mounted lower where they are easier to reach. A large-print cookbook rests on the counter top. Dish colors contrast strongly with place mat and tablecloth color.

And so it goes. Everywhere in the house, products and design features abound that demonstrate practical actions younger and older people alike can take to further enhance aging in place.

EVERYBODY BENEFITS

Of course, many Hartford House visitors have not been older adults. The exhibit has also attracted younger people with concerns about aging parents and older relatives. Perhaps they have a parent living with them and want ideas for modifying their home to make life safer and more convenient for this older person. One of the most interesting of their reactions to the house has been their comments about how many of the features benefit them, too!

They learn, for example, that grab bars in the bathtub enhance safety for every family member, right down to small children. Faucets and shower heads that do not emit scalding water protect everybody.

THE REAL CULPRIT

The Hartford House also helps demonstrate the "quality of life" connection between health and safety. Most contemporary talk on this subject tends to focus on the former. But safety, too, is a quality-of-life issue affected by the design of the physical environment. People—especially older people—often perceive themselves as the culprit when home accidents occur. In fact, the physical environment is more likely to be the culprit. Living spaces that are unfriendly are the problem. They become our adversary in the aging process. The Hartford House illustrates specific techniques for making our living environments our ally.

PRODUCT AND DESIGN INFORMATION

As mentioned, a 90-page pamphlet, *The Hartford House*, is available. Given to every visitor to the house, it describes a wide range of "design tips" and lists the products exhibited, by room, along with their approximate cost and the addresses and phone numbers of the manufacturers and suppliers from whom they can be purchased. A free copy may be obtained by sending a stamped (75¢), self-addressed business-size envelope to The Hartford House, P.O. Box 4460, Hartford, CT 06146.

A half-hour videotape takes viewers on a tour of the house. Titled "For the Rest of Your Life," it includes comments by Pease, Sloan, and two other experts on aging, Robert N. Butler, M.D., chairman of the Department of Geriatrics and Adult Development at Mount Sinai Medical Center in New York, and Patricia A. Moore, who after finishing college, used make-up and clothing to transform herself into an 80-year-old woman and spent three years traveling in the United States and Canada to learn about life from the older person's perspective. The video may be borrowed at no charge by writing to The Hartford House, c/o Modern Talking Pictures, 5000 Park Street, North, Saint Petersburg, FL 33709.

* * *

Beverly Hynes-Grace is assistant vice president, Corporate Gerontology Department, Personal Lines Insurance Center, ITT Hartford Insurance Group.

REFERENCE

AARP, 1990. "Understanding Senior Housing for the 1990s: An American Association of Retired Persons Survey of Consumer Preferences, Concerns, and Needs." Washington, D.C.

Chapter 8

Frail Elders and the Suburbs *

Patrick H. Hare

Single family homes and neighborhoods are the dominant theme of this chapter. Most people who age in the suburbs do so in single family homes, and that is where most of them at least start to grow frail.

Other suburban issues are also discussed, including transportation and how to make civic or homeowners' associations more responsive.

The chapter's italicized assertions are not gospel. The increase in frail elderly people in suburban areas raises too many issues for certainty, and certainty is dangerous—in land use planning, anyway. It should also be noted that low-income frail elders in suburban areas have special needs that go beyond those discussed in this chapter.

A wave of frail elderly people will follow the waves of postwar development out from core cities. After World War II, growth in suburban areas was fed by young households from urban and rural areas. A person who moved to the suburbs in 1950 at age 30 will be 75 years old in 1995. The frail elderly population is not uniformly distributed throughout the United States. It is located in large part in the homes that were built 30 or 40 years earlier. Right now, these are the immediate postwar suburbs.

A wave of frail elderly people aging in place will move through single family areas surrounding older cities. The wave will follow the timing of development, just as a previous wave of school closings did.

*This chapter is based on a longer study available from Hare's firm.

An example can be seen along Interstate 270, which runs northwest out of Washington, D.C., like a spoke from a hub. Here are some aging statistics for the communities along that spoke. In 1990, people over 75 made up 6.4% of the population in Bethesda, an immediate postwar suburb, adjacent to the District line. Next is North Bethesda. Four percent of the population of North Bethesda were over 75 in 1990; 3.8% were over 75 in Rockville, 1.4% in Gaithersburg, and 0.3% in Germantown (Roman, 1990). These figures are shown in a sketch map in Figure 1.

Figure 1. Percent of Population over Age 75, by Planning Area along I-270, in Montgomery County, Maryland.

The figures cited probably do not even show the peak of the wave. In Bethesda, the 6.4 percent figure for persons over 75 in 1990 was followed by 11.3 percent in the age group 65–74 (Roman, 1990).

Suburban single family housing is "Peter Pan" housing, designed for people who will never grow old. To be able to age in place in comfort in an older single family home, a person typically has to be able to go up and down stairs, do simple home maintenance, contract for major home maintenance, drive a car, and enjoy living alone. Most of us will lose one or more of those physical abilities before we die, and probably few of us ever really like living alone.

Alone or not, it appears that medical technology and other factors will keep most of us alive until we have one or more disabilities. A Canadian study, apparently the only one of its kind, indicated that life expectancy for Canadians increased by six years over the period between 1951 and 1978. The punch line is that over 80 percent of the increase, or 4.7 years, was in disabled life expectancy (Soldo and Agree, 1988). Disabilities typically mean home modifications.

The remodeling industry is almost as important to the quality of life of frail elderly homeowners as the healthcare industry. Seventy-five percent of those 65 and older live in single family homes (AARP, 1990a). Eighty-six percent want to "stay in their present home and never move" (AARP, 1990b). If it is accepted, based on these facts, that single family housing is a very common form of elderly housing, then it follows that the remodeling and home maintenance industry is of critical importance to the quality of life of older people.

Frail homeowners will need assistance with major and minor repairs, with routine chores such as changing light bulbs and putting up storm windows, and with installation of ramps, grab bars, and counters for use by people in wheelchairs. In addition, as reported in many studies, older people, not surprisingly, tend to live in older homes. Older homes often require not only more maintenance but also replacement of major items like roofs, furnaces, and hot water heaters (see, for example, Struyk and Soldo, 1980).

Finally, the baby boom has been followed by an empty-nester boom. Our single family housing stock is dramatically underutilized. One-third of the nation's single family homes have enough surplus space to install a complete separate apartment (Hare, 1990). In addition to providing housing for others, the owners of homes with accessory units will also get some combination of added income, security, companionship, and services. To get these benefits, older homeowners will need the assistance of a remodeler.

Choosing to age in place in a single family home has a clear implication: Your remodeler may be almost as important to you as your doctor. The relationship between the frail elderly and the remodeling industry is not an easy one. To begin with, most older homes are a maze of unpleasant pipes and wires and wood. As a result, it is difficult to know whether or not to trust a remodeler. Suppose you hire one to fix a roof, and after starting the job, he or she says, "Well, water got to some of those eaves and rotted them, so we'd better fix them while we're at it." How do you know if they are rotted if you cannot get up there to see them? At the same time, many remodelers feel that older people are not good clients—they will take too long to make up their minds, for example, and even if they do decide to hire the remodeler, will be in the house all day, supervising.

In summary, it is not news that many older people do not trust the remodeling industry and that many remodelers do not want to work with the elderly, particularly the frail elderly. Given that most elderly people want to age in place in single family homes, this mismatch is a little like the dating game from hell.

Three proposals seem worth considering. First, the development of maintenance contracts for homes, much like property management contracts that are used for beach homes and other rental property, would help. They would allow an older homeowner to project maintenance costs and to know that small problems would not become big ones. Second, an independent advisory service is needed to help people select remodelers, draw up contracts, and check for quality of work before making payments. This service exists in Montgomery County (Maryland) and other jurisdictions, but only as a service for low-income people getting subsidized loans for the work. Third, a voluntary neighborhood remodeling committee could help. Made up of retired people who have done remodeling themselves, such a committee would help people find remodelers, prepare contracts, and check quality.

It is possible that one or all of these services already exist. Remodeling for the elderly is only beginning to emerge as a field with its own literature.

Driving should be considered an "activity of daily living," because it is critical to daily living in suburban areas. If they were affordable, chauffeurs would rank next in importance to doctors and remodelers. In most suburban single family homes, driving is critical. Some planners say that Henry Ford not only invented the affordable car, he also invented the single family neighborhood.

Driving should be considered an "activity of daily living," since without it there is no reasonable way to cover the distances created by suburban development patterns. A car and the ability to drive are needed to get to doctors, friends, shops, and almost anything or anywhere but the local elementary school.

Studies that collect data on activities of daily living should include driving. They should probably ask not only if an individual has a driver's license and a car available, but also if he or she feels able to drive without fear on major roads at rush hour, since some metropolitan areas, following the trend of Los Angeles, are approaching close to continuous rush hour conditions. The words "able to drive without fear" are in the question because there are many anecdotes about people who drive despite frailties that limit their driving ability—they simply have no alternative. It should also be noted that most suburban auto trips involve segments on freeways or arterials that assume and require excellent eyesight, hearing, judgment, and response time.

Bus and light rail are not good alternatives for the frail elderly, paratransit (special transportation for frail elders or people with disabilities) is too expensive for more than the most critical trips, and scheduling trips to avoid the rush hour will be increasingly difficult. There are no generally recognized strategies for providing affordable alternatives to the private automobile. Local governments generally cannot provide high quality paratransit for more than the most critical trips to doctors.

It should also be noted that the bus is not a good option for most people, particularly frail people. The average speed of a local bus is about 11 miles an hour, as opposed to 28 miles an hour for the car. The walk, wait, and walk times that are involved in a bus trip lower the speed to about 7 miles per hour. Buses also typically involve the possibility of difficult steps, exposure to bad weather, and delays from traffic congestion (Reno, 1988, Hare 1991a). In addition, Lynn Chaitowitz, an elderly-housing consultant, points out that the time between losing a license because of frailty and being too frail to take a bus is short; in fact, many frail elderly people can probably drive long after they lose the ability and patience to take a bus (Chaitowitz, 1988).

Nor is surburban light rail a solution. As one pundit said, "Mass transit does not work in the suburbs because there is no mass." Suburban densities are so low that most people, including most frail elders, cannot get to stations without a car.

Stories about the legendary congestion of Los Angeles and other cities underline most people's assumption that given a reasonable government and a little planning, congestion should disappear. In practice, transportation planners and community planners may be coming to the conclusion that there is not enough land for the huge roads that will be needed, or enough people willing to have those roads next door to their homes. This is not a politically popular conclusion, but it may be forced to the surface by the Clean Air Act of 1991. If the language of the act is enforced, it may end up being more aptly titled the Transportation Planning Act because of its focus on reducing auto use.

The future of transportation in the suburbs is unclear, but dramatic change will probably be part of it, and that change may help the frail elderly. One of the emerging strategies is HOV lanes, lanes that can be used only by high occupancy vehicles, for example, cars with three or more passengers, van pools, buses. These lanes offer time saving because they are seldom congested. An interesting by-product of this strategy is that as the savings in time or money from using HOV lanes increase, passengers become a highly sought after commodity.

The HOV concept is also beginning to be applied to parking. Either the best spaces or free parking, or both, are given to cars that enter or leave the lot with passengers. It is possible that broad application of the HOV concept to both roads and parking may create a situation in which many cars become free taxis looking for passengers. This is already occurring near HOV facilities in Washington, D.C., in the San Francisco Bay Area, and probably in other regions (Reno, 1988; Hare and Honig, 1990). Free taxis looking for passengers would be of enormous benefit to those, like some frail elderly, who are unable to drive. An interesting application of the HOV idea might be to reserve some of the best parking spots at senior centers for cars that come in with three or more passengers.

However, whether or not the HOV concept can increase mobility for the frail elderly is not yet a serious issue. The concept of free taxis looking for passengers is still a long way from reality for the frail elderly or anyone else, except in a few areas. Nevertheless, the concept illustrates the scale of change that may be coming for many people in suburban areas, including the elderly.

"Traffic calming" is needed for roads, streets, and intersections designed with little consideration for any pedestrian, let alone the frail elderly. Walking is a highly recommended exercise for older people. For

those who cannot drive, walking may not only be good exercise but the only way to get to shops, religious services, and friends. It sounds good, except for one problem. People who cannot drive usually cannot walk long distances, and in most suburban areas, distances are long. Few services are within walking distance, even for a healthy person. In addition, there are few sidewalks, crossing lights, and safety islands for pedestrians, and few shops close enough to get to by walking.

Europeans have coined the term "traffic calming" to cover a variety of means to give more priority to pedestrians. "Traffic calming," however, tends to run counter to the goals of the traffic engineer, whose job for years has been to get as many cars through a given intersection in as short a time as possible. That focus has been fueled by years of complaints about congestion and years of almost no complaints about pedestrian convenience or safety. Concern about congestion has led to storage lanes for lefthand turns at the expense of median safety islands. Safety islands have been thinned to the point where they are more akin to safety razors. Similarly, the timing of "walk" phases on traffic lights seems based on the assumption that there is no one who walks slowly.

Changing the low priority given to pedestrians has become a priority of many transit, bicycle, pedestrian, environmental, and other groups. All are natural allies for aging organizations.

Creating a good environment for pedestrians, particularly those who are frail and old, requires a wide variety of traffic calming devices and many other improvements such as separate pedestrian and bike paths in some locations. A quiet bike creeping up behind anyone at 15 miles an hour is unnerving. It is also frightening to most frail elderly people and can provoke instant rage from parents with toddlers.

All this implies reweaving fine, human-scale threads into a coarse fabric of roads and parking lots developed when the car was king. And as if changing the marching order of traffic engineers was not difficult enough, it will also be necessary to convince an endless number of motorists who have strong opinions about bike paths, reducing turning lanes, or waiting in traffic for a longer walk signal.

Many people think of planning as an exercise in subdividing cow pastures. While cows are not good at articulating their concerns, there are many articulate people in suburban areas who are genuinely concerned about any change in their neighborhoods. Getting involved in traffic calming or other planning issues in suburban communities is like being in an endless soap opera that is only very occasionally successful.

There is, however, some good news. Aging advocates concerned about traffic calming will be welcomed by a large number of allies in the groups mentioned earlier. The welcome will be particularly enthusiastic if the aging advocates make known the number of votes they bring with them.

To reduce isolation in single family neighborhoods, local ordinances or state laws should permit mom and pop shops when owned or sponsored by—or situated in buildings leased from—homeowner or civic associations. Convenience retail is needed in single family neighborhoods, but it has no chance of being permitted under most existing zoning regulations. George Liebmann, a Baltimore land use attorney, has proposed that zoning should permit convenience retail stores in single family zones when they are sponsored by or owned by civic or homeowners' associations (Liebmann, 1990). Management practices such as hours of operation and the number of cars attracted can then be controlled in ways that satisfy the neighbors.

In Garrett Park, Maryland, the situation proposed by Liebmann is a reality. The town owns the building in which the town offices, the post office, a store and deli, a beauty salon, and other small convenience retail establishments are located. The town controls management practices through the leases. It also, at times, has reduced rent to help businesses it feels are important to the community. The town has also fought tenaciously against home delivery of mail, on the grounds that coming to the the Town Center to pick up mail brings the town together as a community. The real estate agent says that the building and its businesses are "the soul of the town." Conversations with the owner of the town store and cafe suggest that this is true. Among other anecdotes about knowing people, she talks about a very frail older woman who lives by herself and comes in for milk. The owner has helped the older woman with her clothes and convinced her that she should not try to carry a full gallon of milk home.

The Town Center is a place where people meet, as is obvious from the numbers meeting inside and outside the businesses on any given day. Unlike the customers at typical convenience retail strip stores, these people all know each other. That, as much as anything to do with convenience, is a way in which older people would benefit from properly controlled convenience centers in existing suburban single family neighborhoods (Hare, 1991b).

As it is, in most single family neighborhoods, there is no place where you meet neighbors. Neighborhoods, in the sense used by Sesame Street and Mr. Rogers, are not common in the suburbs, except on television. The suburban frail elderly probably suffer as much as any group from not being part of real neighborhoods. The clerk in the supermarket express lane may smile, or be clean, or fresh, or live up to whatever slogan management is marketing for the year, but he or she is unlikely to become a friend who asks how your grandchildren are.

Many of the changes in suburban areas that will improve life for the frail elderly will also improve it for everybody else. Universal design is as applicable to community planning as it is to buildings. The changes in suburban fabric needed by the frail elderly will also make life better for many others. Aging advocates, however, can play the leadership role in reshaping suburban areas. Many of the other advocates of change represent groups that by themselves do not influence many votes.

To make change easier, aging agencies and commissions should ask all homeowners' associations to appoint a representative for the frail elderly. At the grass roots of suburbia—in the civic associations and homeowners' groups—the voting power of the elderly is ignored. Typically advocates for the elderly are organized townwide or countywide but have no voice in the neighborhood civic associations. And when an elderly housing project comes up for approval, or when there is a battle over zoning for accessory apartments or over getting a bus route through a neighborhood, it is the civic associations that the elected officials listen to. There may be elderly members who are active in civic associations, but usually they are the healthy elderly, with little feeling for, and perhaps even an unconscious blindness to, the problems of frailty.

In many cases, the first step in starting to improve community planning for the frail elderly should be to have the aging commission ask every civic association to name a representative on elderly issues. It is not a threatening request.

It would also be good for aging commissions to suggest that sister commissions and advocacy groups representing the disabled, single parents, and others make similar requests. These groups often have joint interests in things like pedestrian safety, neighborhood sense of community, and stores you can get to without a car. They also have a similar interest in damping the nay-saying of civic associations that may be dominated by healthy empty-nesters with little understanding of the needs of others.

CONCLUSION

It is simple to say that change is needed. It is also easy to conclude from an article of this nature that our suburbs are curb-to-curb problems and changing them will involve lifetimes of endless and bitter struggle. The suburbs have problems, but the challenges are likely to be easy victories, not sure defeats.

In fact, from the perspective of an advocate for the elderly, the challenge of weaving human scale and contact into the auto-dominated fabric of the suburbs should be attractive. Aging advocates who want to improve suburban communities are in an enviable position. They have a constituency group, the elderly, that is likely to understand very rapidly the ways to improve suburban areas for people of all ages. They can add that constituency to the articulate frustration of environmental groups and others that are beginning to question the highway lifestyle of the suburbs. The votes of the elderly could easily be added to the logic and research of environmental groups and the new generation of transportation planners. If that occurs, there will be few limits to how much finer the fabric of suburban communities can become.

*   *   *

Patrick H. Hare is a Washington, D.C., land use and transportation planner whose firm, Hare Planning and Design, specializes in accessory apartments. He is also a consultant to the National Eldercare Institute on Housing and Social Services.

REFERENCES

AARP, 1990a. "A Profile of Older Americans." Washington, D.C.: American Association of Retired Persons.

AARP, 1990b. "Understanding Senior Housing for the 1990s: An American Association of Retired Persons Survey of Consumer Preferences, Concerns, and Needs." Washington, D.C.

Chaitowitz, L., 1988. Personal conversations with the author.

Hare, P. H., 1989. "Planning for the Frail Elderly in Postwar Suburbs." *Public Management*, July 1989.

Hare, P. H., 1990. "Installations of Accessory Units in Communities Where They Are Legal," Washington, D.C.: Patrick H. Hare Planning and Design.

Hare, P. H., 1991a. Unpublished work based on 1983 National Personal Transportation Survey data.

Hare, P. H., 1991b. Unpublished paper, "A Lesson in the Politics of Getting Convenience Retail Accepted in Single Family Neighborhoods." Garrett Park, Md.

Hare, P. H. and Honig, C., with others, 1990. "Trip Reduction and Affordable Housing." Maryland National Capital Park and Planning Commission, Montgomery County, Md.

Liebmann, G. W., 1990. "Suburban Zoning—Two Modest Proposals." *Real Property Probate and Trust Journal* 25(1, Spring): 1–16.

Reno, A., 1988. "Personal Mobility in the United States," in *A look Ahead:Year 2020*. Washington, D.C.: Transportation Research Board, National Research Council.

Roman, S., 1990. "Demographic Characteristics of Older Residents of Single-Family Homes (in Montgomery County, Md.)." Prepared for the Second Conference on People in Need, December 13, 1990, Montgomery County Planning Department

Soldo, B. J. and Agree, E. M., 1988. "America's Elderly." *Population Bulletin* 43(3, Sept). A publication of the Population Reference Bureau, Inc.

Struyk, R. J. and Soldo, B., 1980. *Improving the Elderly's Housing: A Key to Preserving the Nation's Housing Stock and Neighborhoods*. Lexington, Mass.: Ballinger.

Chapter 9

Aging in Place:
The Role of Formal Human Services*

John N. Morris and Shirley A. Morris

American elders continue to place high value on community residency, with institutional living a viable option only under the most dire of circumstances. For every impaired elder in an institution, there are at least three to as many as five comparable elders in the community. Of all elders who are at high risk of institutional placement during any 12-month period, fewer than one in five will enter an institution. For those who remain in the community despite functional deficits, impaired cognition, and marginal health status, the web of support services must be both complex and continuing. In most cases over the past 25 years, informal supports have assumed the central sustaining role. What was true in the early work of Shanas (1979) and her colleagues remains true today—elders are in the community largely because of the good efforts of their relatives and friends. If this is so, what is the role of formal human services?

Formal service supports have expanded during the last 25 years and today include more publicly provided community services. The allocation of these services to needy recipients has been an issue of considerable interest. Will there be new public entitlement initiatives? Will managed care options take center stage in the public arena? Will

*Research for this chapter was supported by NIA grant #5 R01 AG07820, entitled "High Risk Elders and Community Residence."

long-term-care insurance, with or without public input and control, become a major market force? These are important questions. Yet, whatever the future holds, it is important that we recognize the limited but in some instances crucial role of formal services for elders in the community. We have gone through several decades of seeking to justify formal service provision as a less expensive alternative to institutional residency. We have also sought to use these services either to reduce hospital length of stay or to expedite the rehabilitation or recovery of patients following hospital discharge. There has been very little national attention given to providing such services on an entitlement basis. The combined federal and state programs have varied in their criteria for selecting recipients and for providing care. Medicare and Medicaid programs tend to rigidly control the conditions and extent to which services are available to impaired elders.

New insurance and private entrepreneurial initiatives have to some extent provided alternatives for some elders. Questions concerning either the appropriateness of these programs (e.g., long-term-care insurance) or their cost to the consumer (e.g., continuing care retirement community [CCRC] contract supportive living) raise doubts about the extent to which such programs will have a positive impact on a significant number of elders.

The argument that formal services, when appropriately targeted, can reduce the risk of high-cost institutional placements goes as follows: The risk of impairment status is buffered, informal supporters do not become overburdened or disillusioned, and the overall reality of the individual support network is extended over a wider array of supporters (Wan and Weissert, 1981; Newman et al., 1990; Weissert, 1985). According to this view, informal systems are supported, respite is provided, and the elder remains in the community for a longer period of time. Unfortunately, this view has not generally been substantiated in empirical tests (Berkeley Planning Associates, 1985; Kane and Kane, 1987; Tennstedt and McKinlay, 1986; Kemper, Applebaum and Harrigan, 1987; Weissert, Cready, and Pawelak, 1988; Morris et al., 1987). High-risk elders have been difficult to identify, and when they are identified through outreach efforts, control subjects who are at risk are found to have also been able to secure significant levels of support services. It has been difficult to identify subgroups of impaired elders who would otherwise have received very few services and would have therefore been at imminent risk of institutional placement or death. Nevertheless, limited positive outcomes that have been observed suggest that comprehensive packages can be most advantageous for populations that appear to have self-selected themselves into an institutional path (Sherwood et al., 1981; Ruchlin and Morris, 1983; Brown et al., 1985).

Findings today suggest a model in which the vast majority of persons are able to cope with their difficulties. In most instances, impaired elders do not have to ask for help from their loved ones; it is naturally forthcoming. Even when this has not been the case, most impaired elders indicate that they would be willing to ask their loved ones to come to their assistance (Morris and Sherwood, 1983–84). At the same time, there is a discrete role for formal services, and this is the focus in the remainder of this chapter. Despite the considerable variation and the availability of formal resources, families and impaired elders have been able to incorporate components of the fragmented formal system into the support network that helps maintain these high-risk elders in the community. Distinct patterns of service use have emerged and reflect such factors as residential environment, marital status, the number of informal supporters, risk status, and proximity to death (Struyk and Katsura, 1988; Newman et al., 1990).

NATURE OF COMMUNITY SAMPLE

For the most highly impaired elders as well as for those who begin to decline, living alone becomes a less viable option, and for many, it is the continuation of their marital relationships that translates into the multiple person household. To clarify this phenomenon, we will discuss findings from an ongoing NIA-supported research grant to our team that has permitted us to study a large cohort of elders in the Commonwealth of Massachusetts. First seen in 1982, they are still being followed. The data to be presented here will draw upon information covering the years 1982 through 1987. About 45 percent of all elders report that their spouse is their primary helper. When the spouse becomes active in the support of his or her mate, that individual will become the primary helper in about 95 percent of the cases. Children are more likely to be present as helpers than is the spouse and are a support resource for about 70 percent of all elders. Other relatives are present in one-third of the cases, friends and neighbors in about 25 percent of the cases, and formal services about 10 percent of the time. Over a two- to four-year period about 75 percent of primary helpers will stay the same. Only a small fraction of all elders, less than 5 percent, can identify no informal helpers, while 85 percent can identify two or more informal helpers.

In Massachusetts, three-quarters of all elders live in private homes. The next most prevalent housing setting is private apartments (16%), followed by residency in elderly housing (6%). The oldest cohort is more likely to be represented in housing for the elderly, where over one-fourth are in their eighth decade of life. Over 70 percent of elders in elderly housing and private apartment settings are female, while fewer of those living in private homes are female (55%)——reflecting the much higher proportion of persons in a private home who are married. In accord with these distributions, 85 percent of the residents in elderly housing are not married at baseline. Similarly, two-thirds of those living in elderly housing reported that they lived alone. Following the marital status pattern, the distributions of those living alone in the private apartment and private home settings are 44 percent and 23 percent, respectively. In addition to being older, more predominantly female, less likely to be currently married or to be living with someone else, residents of elderly housing are poorer than their counterparts in other housing settings.

The past two decades have seen the development of a number of different types of housing arrangements, although the actual proliferation of these different alternatives has been less than one would have hoped. A national commitment seems to be lacking, and the unique initiatives in a few states (e.g., Oregon) may have to pave the way for others. Housing for the aged, designed to be barrier-free, with emergency alarm buttons and architectural features that can enhance functioning, has been in operation since the 1960s. Since the 1970s, congregate housing projects have developed, particularly in public housing and in nonprofit-sponsored houses. With barrier-free apartments and common social areas, this type of housing provides its residents with the opportunity to receive, either on-site or in very close proximity, one or more supportive services designed to help maintain independent functioning in a community setting. The level of supportive services varies among such houses, both in type (such as meal, transportation, homemaker, nursing) and intensity of on-site services. Board and care facilities have been in existence for many years, under many names: adult homes, community homes, residential facilities, personal care homes, domiciliary care, and foster care homes, to name a few. These facilities provide housing, food, and some supervision of frail and dependent elderly. They often receive their financing from SSI or state supplemental payments. Shared housing, yet another model, describes living units occupied by at least two unrelated people who share some common living space and is often used by elderly homeowners to supplement their income. Finally, the increase in the number of planned "retirement communities," including continuing care retirement communities, which offer various types of independent living with several levels of nursing care available on the same site, should be noted.

CLIENT SELECTION—WHO SHOULD BE SERVED

Considerable interest has been evinced in identifying individuals who would be appropriate clients for formal service programs in the community. While efforts to specify the unique population at immediate risk of institutional placement have met with little success, a marked advance has been made in our understanding of the parameters under which publicly supported formal services should be provided. There seems to be a broad consensus that more should be done but that it may be unwise to set up a model under which formal services become the primary option of choice for all functionally impaired elders. About 21 percent of all community-living elders are functionally impaired. About 9 percent fit into what could be considered a high institutional risk category (Morris, Sherwood and Gutkin, 1988); about 2 percent have some level of cognitive deficits; and over a two-year period, approximately 3 percent of all such elders will enter a nursing home for either a short or long stay.

Interestingly, while only 21 percent of elders may be impaired, approximately 80 to 90 percent will receive some type of instrumental or personal care service during any one 12-month period. This level of support represents the informal support system at work. Approximately 75 percent of all elders will receive informal support services during a 12-month period. In Massachusetts, for the average person receiving such care, this translates into approximately three-quarters of an hour of support per day. In addition, our Massachusetts data provide no support for the contention that informal support levels decreased during the 1980s.

Given these support levels, one can understand why there has been such an emphasis on targeting formal services to high risk persons. In our work in developing an instrument to identify such persons, the most prevalent set of problems that govern high risk assignment is the presence of multiple activities of daily living (ADL) deficiencies in conjunction with three or more instrumental activities of daily living (IADL) problems for persons 75 years of age or older: 52 percent of high risk elderly had these characteristics (Morris, Sherwood and Gutkin, 1988).

Many investigators have studied this topic. Others have identified elders who are most likely to become recipients of formal services in the community. Given the limited availability of these services, efforts to model current choice practices by elders should be useful in determining the conditions under which publicly provided services may be warranted. From an institutional perspective, while multiple ADL deficits, extreme age, and cognitive decline were primary driving factors, formal choice models have identified an expanded array of personal, social and environmental circumstances that should be considered (Sinclair et al., 1984). Unlike those who use informal supports, the majority of formal support users are functionally impaired. Many have ADL deficits (McAuley and Arling, 1984; Tennstedt et al., 1990), and almost all have limited IADL status (Wilcox and Birkel, 1983; Noam, 1989). Those who seek formal supports in the community are also more likely to have recently experienced a crisis, to have fewer informal supporters, to receive help from friends and neighbors, and less likely to share residence with a caregiver. They also have a tendency to view their informal support services as insufficient (Clark, 1983; Andersen, Kravits and Anderson, 1975; Gross and McMullen, 1983; Noam, 1989; Morris and Sherwood, 1983–84; Penning, 1990). In our studies in Massachusetts, formal supports were more prevalent among elders living in apartments, for persons without a spouse, for persons in high institutional risk status, for those over the age of 80, and for persons being managed by the Massachusetts Home Care Program. The issue of case management has been extensively reviewed. For high risk persons we have found that case management leads to an increase in services irrespective of residential setting. For lower risk individuals, case management appears to increase formal service utilization for apartment dwellers and those who live alone.

Penning (1990) has noted, and our findings tend to support this observation, that a major determinant of formal service use is the prior use of informal support services. It is rare to find a case where an elder began to receive formal services without first having received informal ones.

FORMAL SERVICE UTILIZATION PATTERNS

What level of community support is really required? Given reasonable policy objectives, how much is enough? These questions have appeared over and over again in the literature (Morris et al., 1987; Brody, Poulshock and Masciocchi, 1978; Callahan et al., 1980; Litwak,

1985; Stone, Cafferata, and Sangl, 1987). The question of how to operate formal support services in relationship to informal support networks has been extensively discussed. Some have seen the need for formal daycare and other respite programs. Looking at utilization levels in Massachusetts, approximately one-third of that state's elders will use some type of formal services—in many cases for a limited period of time. On average, formal care recipients are assisted with 1.8 activities—going from 1.6 activities for functionally independent elderly, to 2.3 and 2.9 respectively for elders with IADL and ADL impairments. The two most prevalent areas of support are meals and transportation—38 percent and 33 percent, respectively, of the recipients of formal services are so assisted. In addition to these two services, 17 percent of functionally independent recipients of formal care receive help with housework and personal care, while less than 10 percent receive help with shopping and medication management. For IADL- and ADL-impaired recipients of formal care, approximately 40 percent receive formal help with housework and transportation, while 25 percent of the IADL impaired and 47 percent of the ADL impaired receive help with personal care. Finally, formal assistance with medication management is largely localized to elders who are ADL impaired—averaging 3 percent of the independent, 12 percent of the IADL impaired, and 35 percent of the ADL impaired (Morris et al., 1990).

In assessing formal service use in Massachusetts, one needs to remember that the state has historically had a widespread case-managed Home Care system, although this program has been curtailed to some extent during the recent recession. Under this program, state funds support homemaking, chore, transportation, and other home-based services to approximately 4 percent of elders. It is this market penetration rate on which the prior findings are based, although under its current configuration the program probably reaches about 3 percent of all elders. Our data suggest that significant numbers of impaired elders, particularly those in apartment settings, have been reached by this program. Approximately 70 percent of ADL dependent elders and 50 percent of IADL dependent elders who received formal services were Home Care Corporation clients. For functionally impaired elders residing in private homes, approximately 44 percent of ADL dependent and 23 percent of IADL dependent formal service users were Home Care clients. At the other extreme, for functionally independent (some of whom will have deteriorated over time) users of formal services, homecare participation was at a much lower level—5 percent for those in private homes, 7 percent for those in private apartments, and 14 percent for those in elderly housing (Morris et al., 1990).

The Administration on Aging has historically provided support for transportation and meals programs. Some states, Massachusetts included, have provided extensive networks of homemaking and chore services. Some advocacy groups like the Alzheimer's Disease and Related Disorders Association have pushed for comprehensive health, medical, and psychiatric counseling services for elders in the community. Other programs have a more limited focus on personal care and health-related services. In fact, the latter model underlies the limited Medicare-covered home health benefit. Under this program, this benefit provides ". . . health care services to the beneficiary in the home to maintain health and functional capabilities to forestall the need for hospitalization or other institution-based care" (Silverman, 1990). Unfortunately, use of this benefit has been rigidly controlled in recent years. Silverman reports that the proportion of Medicare-enrolled elders served by the home health agency program rose from 45 to 50 per 1,000 between 1984 and 1988, and the rate has remained relatively stable ever since. Service level is a function of age, going from a low of 30 per 1,000 for persons under 65 to a high of 70 per 1,000 for persons 80 to 84. Since 1988, this program has seen little true growth. For example, in the period from 1983 to 1988, Medicare program payments for this service decreased from 2.6 to 2.4 percent of total Medicare payments.

In the last six years, Medicare has experimented with a new type of comprehensive program, with a more liberal community service benefit—the social/health maintenance organization (S/HMO). This program has been operational in four selected sites. The core service package includes ". . . hospital and physician services with chronic care benefits (e.g., nursing home, personal care, homemaker services) and other expanded benefits (e.g., prescription drugs, eyeglasses, and dental care)" (Newcomer, Harrington and Friedlob, 1990). Service costs are computed on a monthly basis and paid through the health premiums of those who enroll. Unfortunately, the experience and probable benefits from this program will be severely limited in that the proportion of impaired elders enrolled is actually the same or slightly less than the proportion in the community.

Our earlier work, in which we dealt with existing support patterns, revealed that for the cross section of elders in the community, average utilization levels of informal and formal services remain constant over a four- to five-year period for Massachusetts elders (Morris et al., 1990). We see a system in equilibrium. The typical impaired elder is being reached by informal and in some instances formal support resources. As we watch the community over time, some elders oscillate between good and poor status. Others deteriorate and enter the progression leading to death. Informal care represents the prevailing support model and is most prevalent for those sharing a residence with another related (by marriage or blood) or unrelated person and for persons in a private home. Informal support levels increase with resident functional decline, advanced age, and health crises.

The assumption is often made that formal service utilization will continue indefinitely, representing a protracted and unrelenting drain upon the reimbursement system. In fact, this is not the typical model. In our study of Massachusetts elders receiving formal services at baseline, approximately 60 percent were no longer receiving such care at the end of a two-year study. Over a four-year period, approximately 70 percent had stopped receiving formal services. The Massachusetts experience suggests that the model situation is a formal support network that moves in and out of the lives of the elder. To some extent, this may reflect the reality of the federal Medicare home-health benefit and state case-managed homecare benefit. Conversely, it may be an accurate reflection concerning the needs of the community-residing elder. Some elders who were impaired will improve and no longer require support. What was an initial crisis at the time of a new health decline may become the stable model within which the elder lives and for which the informal service system is now able to compensate effectively. Under this assumption, the family and the elder may exclude the formal service workers as soon as possible. There is also the possibility that in the absence of adequate quality control safeguards, some elders are compelled to remove themselves from an ineffective formal care system.

In Massachusetts when formal care services are present, they predominate in less than 20 percent of the cases. They are highest for homecare clients, 60 percent of whom receive more formal than informal care. Formal service levels are also high for elders at risk of institutional placement, as well as elders who reside in an apartment. About one-third of these elders receive more formal than informal care. It is relatively rare for elders to receive only formal care services—only two out of 10 recipients of formal care fail to receive informal supports.

Of those who receive only formal care when first seen, there is a relatively rapid introduction of informal support services. At two years follow-up, 40 percent of these persons will have become informal care recipients. By year four, 55 percent will be informal service users. In fact, by four years, almost half of those who initially were users of formal services will receive more informal than formal care.

There is general support for the idea that the mix of formal and informal services increases for a segment of elders who become increasingly more impaired (Branch and Jette, 1983; McKinlay and Tennstedt, 1986; Stone, Cafferata and Sangl, 1987; Noelker and Poulshock, 1982; Tennstedt et al., 1990). Tennstedt and her colleagues report that the level of care received depends on whether informal or formal help predominates in these mixed mode care situations. Where formal care predominates, the level of total care is significantly lower than it is where informal care predominates. In our work we found that of those receiving a mixture of formal and informal care, approximately one-third were receiving more formal than informal care. They were receiving almost three times as much formal care as the average person in the community, but they were also receiving more informal care than the average for all persons in the community. In fact, their informal support levels are on a par with those who received only informal care. What we observed over time, however, was that informal care levels for this population began to drop and that total care levels for this mixed population began to approximate (over time) the total care levels for those who were receiving only informal care. This reduction in informal support levels is occurring largely for elders living alone in apartment settings. In fact, one of the reported benefits of case management for these elders is a buttressing of the informal support levels in order to reduce and even prevent informal support decline. The observed differential for this mixed care group, as well as for persons in their own homes as contrasted with those in apartments, is probably highly related to marital status. Persons in their own homes are much more likely to reside with a spouse, and the spouse is almost a universal helper when the need arises. The presence of the spouse significantly reduces the need for formal services, and she or he is significantly less likely to cut back on the preexisting informal support levels. When elderly individuals in private homes have a need for ADL support (whether of a personal care or medical nature), there would appear to be a greater likelihood that such care can be provided informally (e.g., Morris et al., 1990).

SUBSTITUTION OF FORMAL FOR INFORMAL

Studies suggest that despite the high volume of informal services provided, there exists a point beyond which families can go no further, and formal care is clearly warranted (Davis, 1978; York and Calsyn, 1977). Under current models, formal service availability has been controlled through a combination of entitlement restrictions and private market payment mechanisms. Many have questioned how our current experience would translate were these restrictions to be lessened. The body of research addressing this topic has been subsumed within the concept of substitution—that is, as formal services are provided, do we see a commensurate and parallel decrease in informal service levels? To study this question, investigators have drawn on a number of different types of information, for example, longitudinal studies of community elders and the unique experience of elders who have been exposed to more generous demonstration programs. To date findings from these efforts provide an unequivocal answer: Substitution is not a common phenomenon. In our analysis of the relationship between changes in formal and informal care over a one-year period for residents exposed to different housing environments and case management programs, formal services do not substitute for or displace informal services but rather serve to support existing informal structures. In the private home or apartment environment, however, it is likely that substitution is occurring—limited, though, to a decrease in the growth of subsequent informal support levels but not a decrease in the average levels observed at baseline.

In 1984, Ward, Sherman and LaGory reported that while "informal networks may serve as lay referrals to formal services, they may also reduce awareness of formal services by substituting for them." In 1985, a Canadian study suggested that the two sources complement each other, with formal sources filling in for the informal when they are absent (Chappell, 1985). In our evaluation of HUDs Congregate Housing Services Program (CHSP), Experimentals received many more hours of formal meal and transportation services (Sherwood and Morris, 1985). On an overall basis, Experimentals received a greater number of hours of formal care than did Controls. This increased formal service utilization could have resulted in a reduction of informal care. On average, Experimentals received two hours of additional formal care in a two-week period over and above what they would have experienced had the CHSP program not been in place. Thus, there was a 24 percent increase in the volume of formal care received. The impact findings with respect to informal substitution were clear. Within the 10 service areas assessed, there was no area of service in which there was a significant Experimental/Control difference in the hours of informal care received. When aggregated as a total figure, Experimentals received 14.7 hours of informal care during a two-week period as contrasted with 14.5 hours for Controls. There is no indication of a significant substitution effect.

Edelman (1986), in an evaluation of the Five Hospital Program, demonstrated that informal services were supplemented rather than replaced by the new formal support services. They indicate that "this finding refutes the notion that community care, in general, replaces informal care with formal services." Interestingly, they also report that over a 48-month period, approximately one-quarter of the primary caregivers had changed. This finding exactly mirrors our findings from Massachusetts. Over a four-year period, 24 percent of the primary caregivers for Massachusetts elders had changed. The likelihood of change was distinctly related to the type of person who was providing the primary help at baseline. The rates of change by type of helper are as follows over a 48-month period: spouse 13 percent, child 25 percent, other relative 36 percent, friends/ neighbor 51 percent, formal helper 75 percent. In our data this represented a shift in who was the primary helper. For the 25 percent of the sample who acquired a new primary helper, in about 30 percent of the cases that helper was a child; in 20 percent, it was a friend or neighbor; and in another 20 percent, it was a formal agency person, with the spouse or a friend/neighbor coming in at about 15 percent each.

In the largest community demonstration of a case-managed homecare alternative to institutional placement—the Channeling Intervention—the issue of formal substitution for informal care was also evaluated. Once again, the investigators failed to see any substantial reduction in informal caregiving patterns (Kemper, 1990).

SUMMARY

We have highlighted a series of key factors to be recognized in evaluating the provision of formal services to elders in the community. Informal resources are a central and pervasive feature in the lives of most elders. Elders begin to receive informal supports before the onset of significant cognitive, functional, or health deficits. Formal care services have been shown to play an interesting companion role for a significant segment of community-residing elders. Only a minority of elders receive formal services. Receipt of those services is highly related to functional deficits and situational problems. The initiation of formal services translates to a predominance of formal care in only a minority of cases. Unlimited formal utilization is rarely a predominant model. Although over 70 percent of elders received informal care, less than 10 percent received only formal care, and only about one-third made use of formal services during a 12-month period. In presenting these data, we believe that they should help temper some concerns regarding how elders will make use of such services. We also believe that these findings help to reinforce the fact that there are subgroups of elders who would unquestionably benefit from participation in a formal service program.

Our review suggests that informal supporters feature prominently in the lives of impaired elders. Findings from the 1980s in no way suggest that this model has significantly changed. Families may be getting smaller, distance may be more of a reality, and female participation in the labor market has undoubtedly increased. Yet, in spite of all of these changes, the role and effectiveness of informal support systems have not undergone a significant change. There remains, however, a need to continue to monitor the possibility that such a change may occur in the future. We have to be particularly vigilant to ensure that any broadening of entitlement to formal service programs in the community does not present a reverse incentive to those who would provide informal care. In this regard, however, a look at the community demonstration programs in operation during the last two decades is most reassuring. Families and other informal caregivers provide help out of a sense of love and duty. We have yet to see a demonstration that was so craftily constructed that it overwhelmed these natural tendencies on the part of loved ones.

*   *   *

John N. Morris, Ph.D., is codirector, and Shirley A. Morris, M.A., is research associate, Hebrew Rehabilitation Center for Aged, Research and Training Institute, Boston.

REFERENCES

Andersen, R., Kravits, J. and Anderson, O., 1975. *Equity in Health Services.* New York: Columbia University Press.

Berkeley Planning Associates, 1985. "Evaluation of Coordinated Community-Oriented Long-Term Care Demonstration Projects." Final Report. Berkeley, Calif.

Branch L. and Jette, A., 1983. "Elders' Use of Informal Long-Term Care Assistance." *Gerontologist* 23:51–56.

Brody S., Poulshock, S. W. and Masciocchi, C., 1978. "The Family Caring Unit: A Major Consideration in the Long Term Support System." *Gerontologist* 18:556–61.

Brown, T. E., Jr., et al., 1985. "South Carolina Community Long-Term Care Project." A Report of Findings Under HCFA Project Grant No. 11-P-97493/4 to South Carolina State Health and Human Services Finance Commission.

Callahan, J. J. et al., 1980. "Responsibility of Families for Their Severely Disabled Elders." *Health Care Financing Review* 2(2): 19–48.

Chappell, N. L., 1985. "Social Support and the Receipt of Home Care Services." *Gerontologist* 25 (1):47–54.

Clark, M., 1983. "Some Implications of Close Social Bonds for Help-Seeking." In B. M. DePaulo, A. Nadler and J. F. Fischer, eds., *New Directions in Helping, Vol. 2.* New York: Academic Press.

Coulton, C. and Frost, A., 1982. "Use of Social and Health Services by the Elderly." *Journal of Health and Social Behavior* 23:330–39.

Edelman, P., 1986. "The Impact of Community Care to the Homebound Elderly on Provision of Informal Care." *Gerontologist* 26:263.

Gross, A. E. and McMullen, P. A., 1983. "Models of the Help-Seeking Process." In B. M. DePaulo, A. Nadler and J. F. Fisher eds., *New Directions in Helping Vo. 2.*, New York: Academic Press.

Kane, R. A. and Kane, R. L., 1987. *Long Term Care: Principles, Programs, and Policies.* New York: Springer.

Kemper, P., 1990. "Case Management Agency Systems of Administering Long-Term Care: Evidence from the Channeling Demonstration." *Gerontologist* 30(6): 817–24.

Kemper, P., Applebaum, R. A. and Harrigan, M., 1987. "Community Care Demonstrations: What Have We Learned." *Health Care Financing Review* 9:87–110.

Litwak, E., 1985. *Helping the Elderly: The Complementary Roles of Informal Networks and Formal Systems.* New York: Guilford Press.

McAuley, W. and Arling, G., 1984. "Use of In-Home Care by Very Old People." *Journal of Health and Social Behavior* 25:54–64.

McKinlay , J. and Tennstedt, S., 1986. "Social Support Networks and the Care of Frail Elders." Final Report to the National Institute on Aging, Grant No. AG03869. Boston: Boston University.

Morris, J. N. and Sherwood, S., 1983–84. "Informal Support Resources for Vulnerable Elderly Persons: Can They Be Counted On? Why Do They Work?" *International Journal of Aging and Human Development* 18:81–98.

Morris, J. N., Sherwood, S. and Gutkin, C. E., 1988. "Inst-Risk II: An Approach to Forecasting Relative Risk of Future Institutional Placement." *Health Services Research* 23:4.

Morris, J. N. et al., 1987. "Formal and Informal Care: Substitution or Not?" Report Prepared under Robert Wood Johnson Grant Number 8136. Hebrew Rehabilitation Center for Aged, Boston, Mass.

Morris, J. N. et al., 1990. "Aging in Place: A Longitudinal Example." In D. Tilson ed., *Aging in Place: Supporting the Frail Elderly in Residential Environments*, Glenview, Ill.: Scott, Foresman.

Newcomer, R., Harrington, C. and Friedlob, A., 1990. "Awareness and Enrollment in the Social/HMO." *Gerontologist* 30(1):86–93.

Newman, S. J. et al., 1990. "Overwhelming Odds: Caregiving and the Risk of Institutionalization." *Journal of Gerontology: Social Sciences* 45(5):S173–83.

Noam, G. 1989. "Implications for Caregiving of the Quality of Elderly Mother– Adult Daughter Relationship." In J. Munnichs and N. Stevens, eds., *Proceedings of the European Behavioral and Social Sciences Research Symposium*, International Association of Gerontology. Berlin: Deutsches Zentrum fur Altersfragen.

Noelker, L. and Poulshock, S., 1982. "The Effects on Families of Caring for Impaired Elderly in Residence." Final Report to the Administration on Aging. Cleveland, Ohio: The Benjamin Rose Institute.

Penning, M. J., 1990. "Receipt of Assistance by Elderly People: Hierarchical Selection and Task Specificity." *Gerontologist* 30(2):220–27.

Ruchlin, H. S. and Morris, J. N., 1983. "Pennsylvania's Domiciliary Care Experiment: II. Cost-Benefit Implications." *American Journal of Public Health* 73(6):654–60.

Shanas, E., 1979. "Social Myth as Hypothesis: The Case of the Family Relations of Old People." *Gerontologist* 19:3–9.

Sherwood, S. and Morris, J. N., 1985, "Impact on Utilization of Informal and Non-CHSP Provided Formal Services." Chapter VI of the Final Report on the Evaluation of Congregate Housing Services Program, in connection with HUD Contract #HC-5373. April.

Sherwood, S. et al., 1981. *An Alternative in Long Term Care: The Highland Heights Story*. Cambridge, Mass.: Ballinger Press.

Silverman, H. A., 1990. "Use of Medicare-covered Home Health Agency Services, 1988. Health Care Financing Note." *Health Care Financing Review* 12(2):113–26.

Sinclair, I. et al., 1984. "Networks Project: A Study of Informal Care Services and Social Work for Elderly Clients Living Alone." Extract from the Main Report. London: Research Unit, National Institute for Social Work.

Stone, R., Cafferata, G. L. and Sangl, J., 1987. "Caregivers of the Frail Elderly: A National Profile." *Gerontologist* 27:616–26.

Struyk, R. and Katsura, H., 1988. *Aging at Home: How the Elderly Adjust Their Housing Consumption Without Moving*. New York: Haworth Press.

Tennstedt, S. and McKinlay, J., 1986. "An Examination of the Interface of Informal Care and Formal Services for Frail Elders." Paper presented at the 39th Annual Meeting of the Gerontological Society of America. Chicago.

Tennstedt, S. L. et al., 1990. "How Important Is Functional Status as a Predictor of Service Use by Older People?" *Journal of Aging and Health* 2(4):439–61.

Wan, T. and Weissert, W., 1981. "Social Support Networks, Patient Status and Institutionalization." *Research on Aging* 3:240–56.

Ward, R. A., Sherman, S. and LaGory, M., 1984. "Informal Networks and Knowledge of Services for Older Persons. *Journal of Gerontology* 39:216–23.

Weissert, W. G., 1985. "Seven Reasons Why It Is So Difficult to Make Community-Based Long-Term Care Cost-Effective." *Health Services Research* 20:423–33.

Weissert, W. G., Cready, C. M. and Pawelak, J. E., 1988. "The Past and Future of Home- and Community-Based Long-Term Care." *Milbank Quarterly* 66:309–88.

Wilcox, B. L. and Birkel, R. C., 1983. "Social Networks and the Help-Seeking Process." In A. Nadler, J. D. Fisher and B. M. DePaulo, eds., *New Directions in Helping, Vol. 3.* New York: Academic Press.

York, J. and Calsyn, R., 1977. "Family Involvement in Nursing Homes." *Gerontologist* 17(6):500–505.

Chapter 10

Aging in Place: The Experience of African American and Other Minority Elders

John H. Skinner

The term *aging in place* can be understood generically as a phenomenon of long-term residency. It is the result of cohort aging in the same place of residence. This is particularly apparent when housing not specifically planned for older persons becomes predominantly elder housing because of the aging of the long-term residents.

At first it may appear that aging in place is race or minority neutral; however, housing is a very volatile area of social relations in the United States, and the problems encountered by racial and ethnic minority elders are very real and uniquely different from those of the majority. The United States has placed high value on neighborhood living, and many neighborhoods have taken on distinct racial and ethnic characteristics. The combination of discrimination and historically low incomes severely limits the choices available to these elders.

This chapter will examine aspects of living arrangements from the perspective of African American and other minority elderly. Circumstances peculiar to these minority elders will be discussed to clarify the concept of aging in place for these groups. Aging in place will be viewed from a cohort, socioeconomic, and geographical perspective. This approach acknowledges that aging in place has personal, family, and community dimensions. Further, this implies that social contextual factors may influence aging in place as much as personal choices.

MEANING OF SHELTER

Shelter is one of the primary needs of human beings; the assurance of adequate housing for the citizenry is one of the fundamental responsibilities of a society. Calmore (1989) cites Achtenberg and Marcuse (1986) who point out that "housing, after all, is much more than shelter: it provides social status, access to jobs, education, and other services, a framework for the conduct of household work, and a way of structuring economic, social, and political relationships." For the elderly, the provision of housing takes on additional dimensions. Simply providing a roof over one's head is not sufficient to handle the more complex needs associated with frailty and disability that accompany old age. They require solutions that provide for a variety of housing options to meet differing needs for shelter. This must range from the options for independent living, through supervised and assisted living, to limited and skilled nursing care.

IMPORTANCE OF LOCATION

Any discussion of housing for African American elders must consider the geographic location. African American and minority elders predominate in inner city areas. Singelakis (1990) reports that the aged living in urban areas constitute more than 60 percent of all older persons in the United States, and 31 percent live in central cities. The elderly make up approximately 11 percent of the inner city population.

ROLE OF INCOME

The amount of income is also important to African American and other minority elders and may affect the value and repair of the housing as well as the neighborhood in which one is located. In fact, for these elders, income may be a more important predictor of the value of housing than of neighborhood location, because of the recurring and persistent discrimination in the real estate market. Ford and colleagues(1990), using data from the GAO Cleveland Study of Older Americans, found that 26.3 percent of white and 41.1 percent of black elders had incomes less than $3,000 a year. Kovar (1988) found that the low rate of income is not only bad but getting worse. She found that black women are the most disadvantaged in terms of income, with 58.2 percent below $3,000 in 1975 and 59.4 percent below $5,000 in 1984.

This extreme disparity in income between the races emphasizes the unique differences facing African American and other minority elders, particularly in inner city areas.

Angel et al. (1991) compared living arrangements of rural and urban elderly and found that black and Hispanic elders were most highly represented in center city areas. Center city elders had fewer living children and were more likely to live alone and least likely to see their children daily than those living in rural areas. Being African American increases the probability of the elderly living in shared arrangements with persons other than their spouses (Soldo, Wolf and Agree, 1990).

LIVING ARRANGEMENTS

It appears that several factors associated with living arrangements may explain different patterns for minorities. Lower incomes of African American and other minority elders may deter admission to nursing homes (Kovar, 1988). There is a large proportion of African American elders who live with spouses and with others, such as relatives and friends (Ford et al., 1990). Choi (1990) found that nonwhite single women, especially widows, are less likely to live alone and that those who do live alone are less likely to be poor. These findings support the notion of the importance of the neighborhood and "community" to minority elderly and the fragile relationship of income, living alone, and aging in place.

The choice of living arrangement and race are not independent of functional status. Soldo, Wolf and Agree (1990) found that severe disability and race were related to living with a child or another person. Even after controlling for income, impairment level, and the number and type of surviving children, African American elders were more likely to rely on coresidence and informal caregiving than were whites. Worobey and Angel (1990) studying unmarried elderly found that African Americans who experienced functional declines were also more likely to remain at home alone than were whites. They also found that Hispanics were less likely to live alone than were non-Hispanic whites. This heavy reliance on informal supports implies a dependence on existing social networks that are more likely to be in place in older, more stable neighborhoods or communities.

Wister and Burch (1987) found that constraining forces influence the ability of a client to cope and make decisions regarding living arrangements. They reported that health status and domestic competence—along with economic feasibility and geographic availability of kin—influence the choice of living arrangement. Ford et al. (1990) suggested that the low rate of institutionalization for African Americans is the result of available social support systems, poverty, and a greater predominance of males among the elderly. A greater proportion of elderly African American males than females have spouses to take care of them. Since these men are more likely than women to live with their spouses, they contribute disproportionately to those with available social supports.

AGING IN PLACE

The concept of aging in place is complex for the African American elderly. African Americans more than any other group in America have been systematically restricted in their choice of where they might live. This long history and persistent problem of housing segregation increases the possibility that African American elders will experience a unique form of aging in place. The combination of economic disadvantage from low incomes, racial segregation, and ageism join to create formidable barriers to housing and the free choice or movement to other housing options.

The problems of housing segregation of other minority persons, while similar, are by no means equal. Calmore (1989), using an index of segregation, found that residential segregation of African Americans was so pervasive that it would take about six decades of average declines of five points per decade in the index of black-white segregation to fall to the current Asian-white or Hispanic-white index ratios.

NATURALLY OCCURRING RETIREMENT HOUSING

Aging in place can lead to naturally occurring retirement housing. As individuals age and continue to live in the same setting, that setting begins to take on the characteristics of retirement housing. The combination of aging cohorts and aging housing stock leads to neighborhoods and communities that take on the identity of retirement settings. This phenomenon is more likely in stable neighborhoods where the residents are likely to grow old along with their housing and neighborhoods. Inner city neighborhoods are less likely to assume retirement community characteristics. These neighborhoods are generally characterized by a bimodal distribution of young persons at one extreme and older people at the other.

Naturally occurring retirement communities may encounter many problems because they were not designed for a retired elder population. Hunt and Ross (1990) summarized previous work on this phenomenon by noting that desired neighborhoods provide supportive living arrangements suitable to the needs and capabilities of older people. They also offer safety and proximity to services and elderly peers. This finding is based on the assumption that older persons have the ability to choose the type and the location of their housing. However, many African American and other minority elders do not have the economic capacity to be able to make these decisions.

Many of the qualities described by Hunt and Ross (1990) are missing in most inner city communities. These communities do not have the infrastructure to support the special needs of their evolved aging clientele. Inner city areas that have become naturally occurring retirement communities have the exaggerated shortcomings of the lack of security and protection, convenient shopping, and transportation. As a result, elders in such areas are isolated and often confined to their homes because of fear and frailty. The combination of surviving to an old age, aging in place, and vulnerability to a hostile environment produces a unique level of existence that is often overwhelming for African American and other minority elders. With few options available to them, they are not only aging in place, they are stuck in place, prisoners in their own homes, without the ability to move to more appropriate housing.

IMPACT OF RELOCATION

Many African American and other minority elders living in inner city areas are also victimized by forced displacement. Calmore (1989) reported that elders, poor people, and nonwhites were disproportionately affected by these displacements. Among the causes for displacement were evictions, mortgage foreclosures, property-tax delinquency, and gentrification. Singelakis (1990) made the point that before the advent of gentrification, 44 percent of elderly residents lived in their housing units for more than 20 years. He reported that the elderly comprise 13 percent of the population of renters in the District of Columbia, but represented 45 percent of those who were displaced by condominium conversions. One of the most startling findings by Singelakis (1990) was that 65 percent of older people would not know where they could go were they to be displaced from their current residences.

CONCLUSION

In conclusion, African Americans and other minority persons face uniquely different experiences throughout their lives as compared to majority persons. These experiences do not disappear with old age; instead, they may become further exaggerated. The combination of years of disadvantage and increasing frailness may create obstacles to the choice of a living arrangement, place of residence, and decisions to relocate. These conditions can become compounded and create situations where minority persons are tied to a geographic area because of low incomes and heavy reliance on informal assistance from relatives, friends, and neighbors. When one cannot afford to purchase the required services or to relocate at will, aging in place may be the reflection of survival in an increasingly inhospitable world. Relocation, especially when forced, may disturb the delicate balance that took years of community living and sharing to establish, resulting in the potential loss of goodwill and social contacts that had been cultivated over many years.

*　　*　　*

John H. Skinner, Ed.D., is associate dean and associate professor, College of Public Health, University of South Florida, Tampa.

REFERENCES

Achtenberg, E. P. and Marcuse, P., 1986. "Toward the Decommodification of Housing." In R. G. Bratt, C. Hartman and A. Meyerson, eds., *Critical Perspectives on Housing*. Philadelphia:Temple University Press.

Angel, J. L. et al., 1991. *Changing Functional Capacity and Living Arrangements of Rural-Urban Elderly*. Presented at the 44th Scientific Meeting of the Gerontological Society of America, San Francisco.

Calmore, J. O., 1989. "To Make Wrong Right: The Necessary and Proper Aspirations of Fair Housing." In J. Dewart, ed. *The State of Black America 1989*. Washington, D.C.: National Urban League.

Choi, N. G., 1990. "Racial Differences in the Determinants of Living Arrangements of Widowed and Divorced Elderly Women." *Gerontologist* 31(4): 496–504.

Ford, A. B. et al., 1990. "Race-related Differences Among Elderly Urban Residents: A Cohort Study, 1975–1984." *Journals of Gerontology* 45(4):S163–71.

Holden, K. C. and Smeeding, T. M., 1990, "The Poor, the Rich, and the Insecure Elderly Caught in Between." *Milbank Quarterly* 68(2): 191–219.

Hunt, M. E. and Ross, L., 1990. "Naturally Occurring Retirement Communities: A Multiattribute Examination of Desirability Factors." *Gerontologist* 30(5): 667–74.

Kovar, M. G., 1988. "Aging in the Eighties, People Living Alone—Two Years Later: Data from the 1984 and 1986 Longitudinal Study of Interviews." *NCHS Advance Data*, No. 149. Hyattsville, Md.

Singelakis, A. T., 1990. "Real Estate Market Trends and the Displacement of the Aged: Examination of the Linkages in Manhattan." *Gerontologist* 30(5):658–66.

Soldo, B. J., Wolf, D. A. and Agree, E. M., 1990. *Journals of Gerontology* 45(6): S238–49.

Wister, A. V. and Burch, T. K., 1987. "Values, Perceptions, and Choice in Living Arrangements of the Elderly." In E. F. Borgatta and R. J. V. Montgomery, eds., *Critical Issues in Aging Policy: Linking Research and Values*. Newbury Park, Calif.: Sage.

Worobey, J. L. and Angel, R. J., 1990. "Functional Capacity and Living Arrangements of Unmarried Persons." *Journals of Gerontology* 45(3): S95–101.

Chapter 11

Aging in Place: Rural Issues

Theodore H. Koff

Any discussion of the aging in place of older persons in rural communities is based on an assumption that aging in rural communities is in fact different from that experienced in urban communities. We must remember, however, that rural communities vary not only in size or proximity to a larger metropolitan area but also depending on whether they are farm or nonfarm, old or new. In addition, there is a wide range of differences among the residents of rural communities, with some having lived in the same place for a long time and others who are recent migrants.

Although many rural communities have a special culture that is based on strong community ties, long history, and ethnic and cultural attachments, these positive attributes are not present in all communities, especially those with predominant migratory patterns or those in severe decline. Residents of some rural communities may have great wealth while others may live in poverty.

Aging in place is a concern for all older persons—those who are affluent, middle-income, or poor—but it is especially a problem for those who are frail and poor. This means there must be an emphasis on older women, because singleness and longevity are of special concern for women. Women live longer than men, spend longer periods in adulthood alone, are poorer than men, and generally are more vulnerable to the problems of aging in rural settings (Fahey, 1988).

However, some limitations on the availability of services in rural communities may equally affect the wealthy and the poor. Some situations may be uniquely complex, as is the case on Indian reservations, where the combination of great poverty, unemployment, enormous distances between homes and services, and absence of a social service infrastructure create very special problems for those who are aging in place.

There also are major uncontrollable events that confront rural communities and can restrict life's opportunities for their residents. Among these are farm failures, out-migration of young people, hospital closures, shortage of health services and personnel, an eroding housing stock, a shrinking tax base, escalating numbers of employees and retirees who lack health insurance, few and overburdened transportation systems, and declining land values (National Council on the Aging, 1990).

All of these issues significantly impinge upon aging in place in rural communities. The ability to age and still remain in the setting of choice, usually the home, rather than be relocated to another community or to an institutional setting, is directly related to the availability and accessibility of resources and services to accommodate increasing infirmity and dependency. And, all too often, increased dependency occurs when no spouse or family member is present, which increases the difficulty of aging in place.

Ideally, an older person should be able to remain in the setting of choice throughout his or her lifespan. Such a choice would be made possible by a community that meets the challenge to provide services that are flexibly responsive to a changing trajectory of frailty and dependency. Since this ideal is far from reality, what are the impediments to the provision of adequate services for the elderly in rural areas?

The National Resource Center for Rural Elderly in 1990 identified seven problem areas that need to be examined in order to understand the difficulties encountered in providing a continuum of healthcare services in rural communities. These are (1) isolation or geographic barriers; (2) economic deprivation or the lack of adequate revenues; (3) lack of a rural human-service infrastructure or the organizational structure necessary to respond to changing healthcare requirements; (4) inability to use economies of scale, with the result that it costs more to provide comparable services in a rural area; (5) lack of a trained labor pool capable of implementing the programs required; (6) cultural antagonism or disparity between expectations of older cohorts and current providers of services; and (7) lack of a consistent, potent advocacy coalition to compete effectively for limited financial resources.

Together, these seven factors illustrate the special problems associated with the delivery of healthcare services in rural communities, and, consequently, each of them contributes to the barriers that make it difficult for the rural elderly to age in place. Each of these factors can be shown to have a particularly significant impact on transportation, healthcare, housing, and family supports—the four service areas that are especially critical if a person is to remain in a place of choice despite changing healthcare requirements.

TRANSPORTATION

Transportation serves as the key to access to the network of services that may be available in a community. Schauer (1991) talks about the decline in rural transportation and its adverse effect on older persons, citing the limited ability of many older persons to continue to drive and the erosion of public transportation resources—those within local rural communities and those linking them to other communities. Limited transportation restricts the ability of older persons to maintain themselves or their households because they cannot shop for food and services or tend to their healthcare needs. How is it possible to age in place without access to basic services? Inadequate transportation facilities can also result in delayed delivery of required medical equipment to the area.

A major obstacle to effective public transportation in rural areas is the high cost of providing door-to-door service and of maintaining bus routes for a few passengers over large geographic areas. Even where limited service is offered during the week, it is highly likely to be unavailable on weekends or holidays. Schauer has pointed out that, in contrast, everyone has postal service six days a week even though the service for rural areas is much more costly than for urban centers.

HEALTHCARE

Critical to the ability to age in place is the availability of responsive healthcare services to meet the changing needs of older persons. In addition to the already-mentioned importance of transportation to enable individuals to reach healthcare services and the added difficulty of finding transportation in rural communities, Coward (1991) has found "that non-farm rural elderly report a higher number of medical conditions, more functional limitations, and a greater number of ADL [activities of daily living] and IADL [instrumental activities of daily living] tasks performed with difficulty" but have less access to healthcare and less help from formal services than are available in large cities.

Rural communities suffer from a maldistribution of healthcare providers and have fewer physicians, fewer specialists, and fewer ancillary service providers. Most of the hospitals that have recently been closed in rural communities have taken with them ancillary services that now can be obtained only by taking long trips to neighboring cities. Increased distances to services combined with limited transportation have resulted not only in reduced access to required care but also in inappropriate or earlier-than-necessary institutionalization or forced relocation to a larger community where the services are available. The readjustments that must be made are not consistent with the goal of enabling an individual who so desires to age in place.

HOUSING

The problems that must be overcome in order to develop specialized housing with services for the elderly, especially those who are poor, are common both to urban and rural areas. Growing numbers of people in need of affordable housing, limited public funds for new construction, constrained budgets for services, and an inadequate pool of experienced administrators are all formidable obstacles to meeting the housing needs of the elderly everywhere, but these are even more serious in rural areas of the nation. The problems were exacerbated in the 1980s by the decline in federal outlays to assist low-income families, and rural housing programs for the elderly and handicapped were especially hard hit, with funding for them declining more than 64 percent (National Council on the Aging, 1990).

Having adequate housing with services for the elderly poor is especially important in rural communities, where a far greater percentage of elders live in poverty (30% as compared to 12.2% of all elders) and much of the housing stock (18%) is substandard (Clark, 1991).

More than one-half of older rural persons live alone, many without transportation or telephone. More than 300,000 rural elderly households lack plumbing, and 1.7 million have no central heating (AARP, 1986). Many who live alone in rural areas are "on farms, in trailers, in hollows, or down dirt roads, where their problems are often hidden from view in a picturesque setting" (AARP, 1986).

Another factor critical to enabling older persons to retain their residence in a rural community is the availability of home health, homemaker, personal care, and transportation services either furnished as part of a housing program or available from the community. Approximately 80 percent of rural older persons own their own homes, but a large percentage live in substandard housing. Additional efforts have to be directed toward maintaining these households in safe, reliable condition, toward finding ways to accommodate groups of elderly people in underutilized old homes, and toward making services available to meet their changing needs.

FAMILY SUPPORTS

For many individuals the ability to age in place depends upon supportive services provided by family members and neighbors. As younger family members have moved away from rural communities, the social support networks have become smaller and not as readily available (Stone, 1991). Primary caregivers in rural areas are more likely to be spouses and to have lower incomes than their urban counterparts (Stone, 1991). Neighbors may not live in close proximity, may not have transportation, and may themselves be older and in need of the caregiving rather than being able to provide the service. In many rural communities there may thus be a greater need for formal services because of the absence of a range of informal supports.

CONCLUSION

In conclusion, it appears that the difficulties of aging in place in rural communities stem from government policies that reflect little or no interest in enabling older persons to age in place in their residence of choice. If older persons want or require a continuity of services, they must relocate to a larger community. Such a policy stance is totally out of keeping with the following stated goals of the Older Americans Act, which are to provide "a comprehensive array of community-based, long-term care services adequate to appropriately sustain older people in their communities and in their homes" and "efficient community services, including access to low-cost transportation, which provide a choice in supported living arrangements and social assistance in a coordinated manner and which are readily available when needed, with emphasis on maintaining a continuum of care for the vulnerable elderly" (U.S. Congress, 1989).

Concern for people as manifested in services for the elderly should not be restricted to urban areas. Yet the denial of sufficient funds to overcome the handicaps noted in this paper has resulted in a de facto policy of providing people who live in rural areas with less public support than is provided to those in urban areas.

It is, of course, not feasible to duplicate all of the sophisticated technology found in tertiary care hospitals in every community hospital, and there are ample illustrations of how it is possible to be more responsive to highly technical needs in large communities than in rural environments. Yet when it comes to basic requirements (i.e., transportation, healthcare, housing, and caregiving), a basic obligation to "sustain people in their own communities and their home" has not been fulfilled. Just as mail is delivered to rural residents even though the delivery costs are higher than those in metropolitan areas, so should equity be ensured for older persons who live in rural communities and need basic services to enable them to age in place.

*　　*　　*

Theodore H. Koff, Ed.D., is professor, School of Public Administration and Policy, and director, Long Term Care Program, Arizona Center on Aging, College of Medicine, both at the University of Arizona, Tucson.

REFERENCES

AARP (American Association of Retired Persons), 1986. *After the Harvest: The Plight of Older Farm Workers*. Washington, D.C.

Clark, S., 1991. "Housing." Presentation at the National Symposium on the Future of Aging in Rural America, July. Kansas City, Mo.: National Resource Center for Rural Elderly.

Coward, R. T., 1991. "Improving Health Care for Rural Elders: What Do We Know? What Can We Do?" Presentation at the National Symposium on the Future of Aging in Rural America, July. Kansas City, Mo.: National Resource Center for Rural Elderly.

Fahey, C., 1988. "Housing for the Future." *Journal of Housing for the Elderly* 5(1): 3–4.

National Council on the Aging, 1990. *Perspectives on Aging* (March/April). Washington, D.C.

National Resource Center for Rural Elderly, 1990. *The Rural Elderly Networker* 2 (4, July 15). Kansas City, Mo.

Schauer, P., 1991. "Access and Transportation Implications for the AoA Network and Recommendations for the Future." Presentation at the National Symposium on the Future of Aging in Rural America, July. Kansas City, Mo.: National Resource Center for Rural Elderly.

Stone, R. I., 1991. "Rural Caregiving: Implications for the Aging Network." Presentation at the National Symposium on the Future of Aging in Rural America, July. Kansas City, Mo.: National Resource Center for Rural Elderly.

U.S. Congress, 1989. *Compilation of the Older Americans Act of 1965, as Amended through December 1988.* Washington, D.C.: Government Printing Office.

Chapter 12

Supportive Services in Senior Housing: New Partnerships Between Housing Sponsors and Residents*

Susan C. Lanspery

Older residents[1] of federally assisted housing are among those with the fewest resources to age in place successfully. Increasing proportions of residents are over 75 and likely to be frail. Many lack or are isolated from family and have incomes too low to purchase desired services at market prices. Fellow residents may be disinclined or unable to provide assistance because of their own frailty or lack of community feeling. Access to publicly financed services may be compromised by isolation, ignorance, rigid eligibility requirements, and limited program resources. Further, residents may be reluctant to seek services, fearing eviction or stigmatization, given housing programs' requirements that they be able to live independently.[2]

[1]Throughout this chapter, people who live in federally assisted housing will be called residents; those who develop and own housing developments, whether individuals or syndicates, owners; those responsible for management, whether management companies or on-site staff, managers.

[2]Many of these problems were confirmed in market research conducted by Supportive Services Program in Senior Housing grantees.

*Presentation of this chapter was assisted by grants from the Robert Wood Johnson Foundation. The views expressed are solely those of the author. Official endorsement by the Robert Wood Johnson Foundation is not intended and should not be inferred.

One might expect housing sponsors themselves to address these problems and help residents to age in place. Indeed, service providers, residents, and families often make the assumption that senior housing offers both services and support. In practice, however, this is usually not the case. Historically, federal and state housing policies have held housing sponsors accountable only for physically and fiscally sound dwelling units and have required that residents live "independently." Such policies implicitly discourage housing sponsors from involvement in service provision or access. Although many managers nevertheless provide support, assistance is far from universal and tends to be unsystematic. Managers often lack the resources and expertise necessary to ensure service adequacy, and they may be as overwhelmed as residents by difficulties in gaining access to services.

In 1988, the Robert Wood Johnson Foundation initiated a demonstration aimed at changing this situation. The Supportive Services Program in Senior Housing (SSPSH) is expected to generate consumer-driven services and new revenues from resident payments, development funds, and housing finance agency funds. Services are intended to reflect residents' preferences, rather than others' judgments as to what residents ought to have. An implied goal is to change housing sponsors' perspective that housing is strictly "bricks and mortar."

Through the SSPSH, 10 state housing finance agencies (HFAs)[3] have integrated supportive services for older people into over 275 HFA-financed (usually federally assisted) housing developments. Services are now available to 35,000 residents in these developments. HFAs, the developments, and 10,000 residents have spent over $3.5 million in new revenues on these services. The SSPSH has shown that HFAs, development owners, and housing managers can and should be added to the potential service resources available to older people.

NATURE OF THE DEMONSTRATION

The three-year demonstration began in November 1988, with planning grants to HFAs in Colorado, Illinois, Maine, Massachusetts, New Hampshire, New Jersey, Pennsylvania, Rhode Island, Vermont, and Virginia.

---

[3]HFAs, public or quasi-public agencies or authorities, finance low- and moderate-income housing and sponsor other programs.

The HFAs' first implementation task was to "market" the SSPSH idea to owners, managers, and residents. HFAs asked these groups about their concerns about services, conducted market surveys to learn resident preferences for services, and researched community service availability and costs. Among other findings, the HFAS found that managers, owners, and residents share an interest in services that help residents to maintain independence and control, such as housekeeping and transportation. Using this information, HFAs were able to promote the expected advantages of participation to the three target groups.

• HFAs appealed to owners' altruism as well as self-interest. Some owners were swayed by the HFAs' documentation of service needs and desires and their own or their managers' knowledge of residents' problems. Others wanted to know the expected return on their investment in a supportive services program. To that end, HFAs portrayed a supportive services program as a way to promote resident independence, support managers, reduce manager and resident turnover and associated costs, and improve building maintenance, management-resident relationships, and the development's marketability.

• Similar persuasion appealed to managers. They were, of course, especially interested in the notion that a supportive services program could reduce pressure on themselves and other staff members, enhance their ability to keep residents independent, and help them to take better care of the building. In the words of one project director, "They recognize now that supportive services preserve the building as much as paint does."

• Residents responded to reassurance that management was endorsing services and that the demonstration could help them to stay independent. HFAs and developments conveyed the notion that using supportive services is not a reflection of weakness but a wise purchase. Residents participated in designing and maintaining services through market surveys, focus groups, "voting with their wallets" for services, and resident associations. Residents were encouraged to "own" the services and share responsibility for the service programs' success.

PROGRAM CHARACTERISTICS

Table 1, prepared by the independent evaluators at the Georgetown University Center for Health Policy Studies (see chapter by Feder,

Table 1. RWJF Supportive Services Program in Senior Housing
Number of Users, Units of Service, and Units per User
May 1990—April 1991

| | Users | | Units | | |
	Number	Percents of Tenants	Number	Percent of Total Services	Units Per User
Service Coordination	5,050	25.0	24,901	9.5	4.9
Light Housekeeping	1,985	9.8	51,297	19.6	25.8
Chore	1,668	8.3	13,022	5.0	7.8
Transportation	2,169	10.8	36,778	14.1	17.0
Meals	2,160	10.7	99,280	37.9	46.0
Shopping/Errands	532	2.6	8,307	3.2	15.6
Health Services	280	1.4	1,559	0.6	5.6
Personal Care	890	4.4	26,488	10.1	29.8
At Least One Service	9,799	48.6	261,632	100.0	
At Least One Service, Excluding Service Coordination	7,105	35.3	236,731	90.5	

Note: This table is based on a sample of 186 developments. A unit equals one hour for all services except transportation and meals, where a roundtrip and meal respectively equal one unit.

Scanlon, and Howard, this volume), illustrates the kinds of services provided and frequency of use in the participating developments. The main services—service coordination, housekeeping, chore, transportation, and meals—reflect the interest expressed in the initial market research. Although program activities differ considerably across and even within states, the following broad characterizations are possible:

First, service coordination is a key element in most sites. It is often performed by a development employee or someone with whom the development has contracted. Some developments have their own full- or part-time service coordinators; others share; and still others assign service coordination functions to on-site housing managers. HFA staff may play a major role in a development's initial program activities, such as negotiating with service providers, with day-to-day service coordination tasks being carried out by the on-site manager.

Second, service coordination is consumer-oriented, has a strong brokering function, and is geared to serving the overall resident population as well as specific resident requests. As one HFA staff member put it, "It is up to the service coordinator to express the personality of the development." The coordinator's primary role is to ensure that services residents want are available and affordable. Tasks include the following:

- Initial research on and regular monitoring of residents' preferences.
- Brokering affordable or free services using economies of scale to get a lower price; promoting residents as a potential market and the development as a site for seminars, health screenings, recreational programs, etc.; and helping residents obtain services for which they are eligible.
- Managing or helping to oversee on-site services (e.g., housekeeping, transportation).
- Helping residents to obtain equipment like grab bars and negotiating with the manager for modifications like lever handles, user-friendly locks, and lower peepholes.
- Increasing residents' disposable income, through SSI, Medicaid, food stamps, and other programs, or discovering that residents have allowable deductions to income (which lowers their rents)—thus making money available to purchase services, if desired.
- Working closely with resident groups to obtain their input on services and to help strengthen the resident community; responding to residents' desires for informal support, meaningful participation, and better problem resolution.

Third, while it is less common for developments to finance services other than service coordination, many developments have established other services in response to resident interest: More than 85 offer housekeeping and heavy chore services, more than 60 offer transportation or shopping assistance or both, and more than 35 offer meals. In some cases, developments pay or subsidize salaries of housekeepers or drivers. In others, developments do not finance the services but help to make available—through contracts, other agreements, or service coordinator initiation and oversight—discounted services that residents purchase themselves.

Fourth, most of the financing for service coordination and other new services comes from allowing developments with adequate resources and flexibility to use operating budgets or residual receipts for service-related activities.[4]

Fifth, most HFAs were surprised at the extent to which managers already accommodated aging in place and at the strength of owners' interest in becoming involved in services. As one project director said, *"They* were wondering when *we* were going to do something."

Sixth, resident isolation is a significant factor in many developments. Over 80 percent of residents live alone. About one-third have no living children. Many residents leave their buildings only a few times per month. According to managers and service coordinators, many residents do not know their neighbors. Most developments had no active resident association at the start of the SSPSH, and those associations that existed were all too often dominated by a small group.

HIGHLIGHTS

This section offers a few examples of resident involvement, keeping costs low, and ways in which the program has changed the lives of participating individuals.

Residents have been involved in service planning in a number of creative ways. For example, in Maine, residents held a "taste-testing" competition for a food service contract. The service coordinator arranged for a consultant to help the residents develop criteria for their decision. In Vermont, residents initiated and established, with the assistance of the service coordinator, a 501(c)(3) nonprofit corporation that will be the framework for adding new services to the development. The group's first goal is to raise funds to start up and subsidize a heavy-chore service for which residents will pay a discounted fee.

Owners and managers have also been creative in adding services while keeping costs down. For example, some developments extended

[4]Most of the developments participating in the SSPSH are known as "pre-1980," "pre-universe," or "old regulation" Section 8 developments. For these developments, the use of residual receipts must be approved by the HFA but is less restricted than in later Section 8 developments.

part-time custodians' hours so that they could perform affordable heavy-chore services. Others have been willing to work with other developments to provide services. For example, one development with adequate resources purchased a van and reached an agreement to share it with a neighboring development. Residents' fees cover most of the operating costs.

Some of the more dramatic differences in participants' lives tend to occur when the program helps residents become less isolated. In the words of an observer, "A dying building becomes a living building." Stories of both revitalized resident associations and reinvigorated individuals are common. For example, a previously defunct resident association was built up with help from the service coordinator. When the coordinator left a year later for another job, a committee of eight residents wrote a letter to management—with thirty cosigners—expressing their appreciation and their (very assertive) hope that a new coordinator would be hired soon. In another example, a resident had not ventured from her development on her own in years and, in fact, had rarely left even with an escort. After some persuasion by the service coordinator, she took a development-sponsored trip, became a frequent user of the new development transportation service, and eventually became involved in the resident association. Another resident took on an active community role after she responded to the service coordinator's invitation to help with the gardening, a lifelong avocation that she had given up most reluctantly when she moved into the building. Still another resident resumed a leadership position in the resident association. Thanks to the development's new, affordable chore services, she was able to say, "My apartment looks nice enough to invite the neighbors in again."

CONCLUSION

SSPSH participants have built on the experience of other types of housing integrated with services, such as congregate housing and life care communities. They have also been innovators. No one HFA's experience may be completely replicable, even to another HFA, but the SSPSH experience reinforces the growing enthusiasm for integrating housing and services. It has much to offer such efforts, especially in addressing housing sponsor roles; encouraging resident participation; developing enhanced, facility-wide service coordination; financing; and organizing service delivery.

ACKNOWLEDGMENT

The author wishes to thank James Callahan, Judy Feder, Bill Scanlon, Stephen Somers, and the SSPSH project directors for their assistance in preparing this chapter.

*   *   *

Susan C. Lanspery, Ph.D. is a senior research associate at the Heller School, Brandeis University, and the SSPSH deputy director.

Chapter 13

Supportive Services in Senior Housing: Preliminary Evidence on Feasibility and Impact*

Judith Feder, William Scanlon, and Julia Howard

In addition to its sponsorship of the Supportive Services Program in Senior Housing (SSPSH) (described in Lanspery, this volume), the Robert Wood Johnson Foundation has supported an independent evaluation of the program's implementation and experiences. The evaluation's fundamental objectives are to determine (1) whether and under what circumstances supportive services programs consistent with the principles described previously can be implemented and sustained, and (2) what impact such programs have on elderly tenants, the housing developments, and the sponsoring housing finance agencies (HFAs). While still under way, the evaluation's preliminary evidence indicates that, subject to some qualifications, the demonstration will achieve its broad goals of developing services that can be sustained beyond the life of the demonstration. Further, the potential seems to exist to extend service programs to other HFAs and housing developments. With its demonstration, the Robert Wood Johnson Foundation seems to have identified a concern about support for people aging in

*Preparation of this chapter was assisted by a grant from the Robert Wood Johnson Foundation. The views expressed in this chapter are solely those of the authors. Official endorsement by the Robert Wood Johnson Foundation is not intended and should not be inferred.

place—a concern shared by HFAs and many developments—and to have provided the focus and tools to address that concern in a way likely to become institutionalized over time.

DEMONSTRATION EXPERIENCE

The first evidence for these conclusions comes from the experience of the participating HFAs. Interviews indicate that the demonstration enabled HFA leadership and staff to initiate or expand activities in a way that would not have occurred had the demonstration not been present. Although HFA's were definitely aware of problems their developments face in housing aging tenants and some had even begun to explore or develop a capacity for ensuring access to service, none had undertaken the concentrated commitment that the demonstration made possible. The demonstration enabled senior management and others within HFAs to mobilize sufficient management attention, resources, and staff to build and institutionalize a service responsibility within the HFA. In sum, the demonstration legitimized and encouraged HFA attention to issues that went beyond safe and financially sound housing.

Furthermore, the demonstration enabled HFA staff to move owners in the same direction through mechanisms like the following:

* Apprising housing developments of service availability.
* Surveys of tenants to determine the kinds of services they want and would be willing to pay for.
* Training and technical assistance for managers and service coordinators to facilitate operations on their own.
* Recognition of service coordination and other costs in operating budgets, to provide financing for these activities.
* Encouragement of copayments and other mechanisms to alleviate owners' fears that service commitments could place "excessive" demands on their resources.

Not only have HFAs undertaken these activities as part of the demonstration, they have also incorporated into their normal housing management oversight of development operations in a variety of ways. First, most have made or expect to make the demonstration project director's position permanent. Second, they are considering ways to require or encourage the developments in their portfolios to be accountable for services to their tenants. Third, they recognize and intend to promote financial and management officers' awareness of and sensitivity to tenants' service needs as part of overseeing development operations.

Owners' behavior provides similar evidence of change. In most states participating in the demonstration, the idea that aging tenants pose management problems was fairly prevalent when the demonstration began. Although most HFAs could identify individual developments that had undertaken some service initiatives before the demonstration began, they did not see them as typical. On the contrary, the prevailing view was that owners knew a problem existed but had no sense of their responsibility for addressing that problem or of mechanisms that could address it, were they willing to pursue them.

In this context, the HFAs' job has been to make clear both that owner responsibility does exist and that it can be addressed to the financial benefit of—or, at a minimum, without financial detriment to—the owners they work with. Although the evaluation is still in the process of collecting information from developers, managers, and service coordinators, contacts to date suggest that development managers—in management companies and on-site—have been prime movers in persuading owners that this is the case. As the "front line" in serving aging tenants, managers tend to see the value in the support the demonstration provides: first, by the presence of staff dedicated to developing a system for providing tenants assistance; and second, by that system's ability to prevent tenants' personal needs or crises from becoming management crises.

Managers report that service coordination and availability can help avoid damage to or decline in property value, improve relations with and quality of life for tenants, and allow managers to devote more time to the tasks of building management, with which they are more comfortable. Such beneficial results enable them to convince owners that service-related activities are a good idea. Key to managers' ability to make this case have been HFA signals that service activities are appropriate. HFA support has meant that managers do not have to actually prove to their owners that service support will improve bottom lines (for example by preventing damage or reducing tenant turnover). They have simply had to demonstrate that a service capacity can make everybody better off at little or no financial risk.

With respect to continuation of these activities, owners and managers have expressed uncertainty on two counts: (1) HFAs' commitment to sustain the technical assistance that developments have come to count on, and (2) the continued availability of mechanisms used to finance service activities. As indicated above, HFA attitudes suggest that the first uncertainty can easily be laid to rest. Regarding the second, some managers are concerned that HFA authorizations to include service coordination in operating budgets were a temporary phenomenon. If HFAs put these concerns to rest by making their commitment to continued support explicit, owners and managers, too, are likely to remain committed.

CONCLUSIONS

Assessed in terms of its capacity to extend HFAs' and housing owners/managers' attention beyond bricks and mortar to service needs *and* in terms of its probable impact beyond the demonstration period, preliminary evidence indicates that the Robert Wood Johnson Foundation Supportive Services Program in Senior Housing has been a success. But the foundation's objectives for the demonstration go beyond that. Will a service orientation go beyond the already involved housing developments in the participating states? Will other states follow the path of participating HFAs?

Although neither question can be answered at this stage, each has some legitimacy. It is certainly possible that the developers HFAs have been able to attract differ from others in the state. It may be that other developments will require far "harder" evidence that services make financial sense or will be unwilling to involve themselves in services under any circumstances, believing simply that it is not their job. Furthermore, not all developments have sufficient resources to support service activities, even given the facilitating mechanisms HFAs have offered. It may be, then, that there is a limit to supportive services in subsidized housing, although we do not yet know what that limit is.

Similarly, there may be a limit among HFAs. Just as participating developments may differ, participating HFAs may differ from those in other states. Others may be less ready or willing to assume responsibility for services and may prefer simply to stay with the financing and oversight tasks with which they are familiar. Again, it is premature to speculate on whether or not this is the case.

Perhaps of more concern to future policy than these issues of institutional change is the impact the demonstration's investment in service capacity has on the residents of subsidized housing. Unassessed is whether shifting the focus of housing agencies and developments beyond bricks and mortar actually makes residents better off. Impacts on residents are, of course, difficult to measure. Preliminary contacts with managers and service coordinators indicate, however, that they believe the availability of service has indeed improved residents' quality of life, not only by providing individual residents access to services they may want or need but, equally important, by increasing residents' confidence, comfort, and sense of community in participating buildings. Here too, however, there may be limits to the support developments are willing or able to provide. Although an emphasis on service coordination rather than specific services may alleviate owner concerns about expenditures going "out of control," such emphasis may mean an inadequate supply of certain kinds of services residents cannot obtain on their own.

In sum, preliminary evidence suggests that the Supportive Services Program in Senior Housing is making a difference to HFAs, developments, and their residents and that there is a potential for extending and expanding that impact beyond the demonstration participants. At the same time, there is evidence that there may be limits to future growth. Both potential and limits will be further explored as the demonstration comes to an end and the evaluation moves toward completion.

ACKNOWLEDGMENT

The authors wish to thank James Callahan, Susan Lanspery, Andrea Kabcenell, and Stephen Somers for their comments.

*   *   *

Judith Feder, William Scanlon, and Julia Howard are from the Georgetown University Center for Health Policy Studies, which is conducting the evaluation of the SSPSH.

Chapter 14

Aging in Place From North to South

Margaret Clemons

Turning daydreams into reality resulted in my relocation from Cambridge, Massachusetts, to the South when I retired. In deciding where I would go, I followed the usual process, reviewing travel opportunities, housing options, and the climate, demography, and community trends of various places. Mother enjoyed sharing this process, and I was convinced that she would make the move with me. However, as I narrowed my choices to a particular area, she became less and less interested. Finally she informed me that at age 91, she was not about to make any move and would much prefer that we exchange frequent visits. I selected a small city in South Carolina. Mother and my sister, the oldest of three girls, helped me prepare for my move. Finally, the last week, when all was packed, Mother said that she would take the trip with me, as I should not drive that distance alone. We could also stop over in Pennsylvania with my other sister, the youngest. I was so happy, and I just knew that she would love South Carolina, once she was there, and want to stay.

I am not at all certain that I would have made the transition without her. She planted onions, which "must go in early." Time moved quickly with so much to be done, and while we didn't know anyone in town, I cannot remember being lonely. After five weeks she said it was time for her to go home. We had our first real rain on the day of her leaving, and I cried along with the windshield wipers all the way home alone from the airport.

Two years later, at age 93, Mother needed a permanent home base instead of being shuffled among sisters. She decided to come and live with me in my big two-story house.

These days, Mother and I have plenty of room for family visitors. She goes up and down stairs carefully at least eight times a day, more for the exercise than anything else. Shopping was our major outing until Mother enrolled in the elder daycare program. Now when we go to special events, there is always someone who knows her from the Rice Center Day Care Program. Their big social has become the annual Valentine Ball held at the Calhoun Senior Living Center, which is the renovated old hotel that formerly was the site of all the city's social affairs. High school students act as escorts for us seniors, and Mother is probably the most senior of all who have attended the ball. As her director says, she seems to enjoy the events she attends with me.

We have a small group of closer friends who share good times together for birthdays and holidays. We visit other elders who are not able to get out and about, but this is somewhat depressing for her. In fact, our first visit to a nursing home truly confused her when we had such a long waiting time before we could see our friends. She'll be 99 this year and is proud of her good health—no aches or pains and no medications, and a good bill of health from her doctor's examination. "I just can't remember things from one time to the next, and I live for the present," she says. Yet, like most older persons, she loves to recall her earlier days—the time the blustery storm caught her riding alone in the horse-drawn buggy on her way to her grandmother's house, for example.

Until this year, I attended board and committee meetings of the Older Women's League held in Washington, D.C., for two to four days. The first time I went away we hired a homemaker to stay with Mother. Upon my return, she assured me that she did not need anyone to stay with her again as she is capable of keeping house alone when I am away. And that she did for my following meetings. I missed only one in five years for feeling unsure about her and used only telephone contact and the drop-in service of a neighbor to assist her during my absence.

We always keep a jigsaw puzzle going. We must enter her recipe for grated sweet potato pudding for the power company calendar. She also makes a superb apple pie. Now that spring seems to be here already, we'll spend more time outdoors on foot, looking for the daffodils, tulips, and magnificent camellia flowers and, soon, the dogwood blossoms. Then summer, with the sweet scent of magnolias and the visits of the grands and great-grands. She also has two great- great-grandchildren.

She'll play games and cuddle the little ones and tell them all about her buggy ride in the storm. So life goes on for both of us here in the South.

*   *   *

Margaret Clemons is the former assistant secretary of the Massachusetts Department of Elder Affairs and is a past vice president of the Older Women's League. She and her mother now reside in Anderson, South Carolina.

Chapter 15

The Bay Area Independent Elders Program: Community Support as a Resource for Aging in Place

Lori Andersen

Can a community rally to create more support and sensitivity for frail elders aging in place and the people who care for them? Do resources not traditionally considered exist to supplement what is available through formal services? Can local businesses, churches, service clubs, and others be tapped to expand the base of support for frail elders? Will community coalitions work to identify problems facing this population and to advocate effectively for systems change? Three years after the Bay Area Independent Elders Pro- gram (BAIEP) was launched, 11 communities in and around San Francisco have demonstrated that the answer to all of these questions is yes.

- In Berkeley, local businesses and over 700 volunteers joined forces through the donation of materials and their labor to improve the safety of 22 elders' homes. Across the bay on the coast side, a local building contractor works part-time with the Independent Elders Network to direct a similar home repair project for frail elders. Volunteers repair stairs, heating, lighting, and plumbing, and build ramps, clear yards, and haul debris.
- A "social worker's beat" was created in Bayview–Hunters Point, San Francisco's largest African American community, putting a

social worker in weekly contact with the local stores, banks, pharmacies, physicians' offices, and churches that elders frequent. These relationships help to identify elders with needs and link them with aging services.

- Coalition advocacy efforts in one community resulted in an important change to the paratransit system—the elimination of geographic boundaries set by individual cities that fund and operate their own special-needs transportation services. This took away a major barrier to frail elder participation in the paratransit program and subsequently their use of other resources in the community.

- "Gatekeeper" type programs in San Mateo, West Contra Costa County, Morgan Hill, and other sites have mobilized resources like bank personnel and firefighters to become the "eyes and ears" for community outreach efforts.

- In San Mateo County, a single well-publicized telephone number connects elders (and others) with professional case managers on a 24-hour-per-day basis.

GUIDING PRINCIPLES

The sponsors of BAIEP—the Henry J. Kaiser Family Foundation, the Koret Foundation, the San Francisco Foundation, and the Marin Community Foundation—have created a program to mobilize the different sectors within a community to work together to create, strengthen, and expand options for frail elders and their caregivers. The program is guided by the following set of beliefs: that elders prefer to live in their own homes and can do so if appropriate assistance is available; that a number of obstacles restrict elders' access to available services; that many of the needs of frail elders can be met in the community by informal resources; that coordination between the informal resources and the formal service system is key to the development of a responsive, overall support system; and finally, that involvement of elders and the broader community in the planning and direction of services will strengthen the capacity of that community to respond appropriately to the needs of elders.

COMMUNITY COALITION

The core of the 11 grantee projects are the coalitions made up of formal service providers, elders, their family and friends, advocacy groups, public officials, service clubs, local merchants, and religious organizations. Funded by BAIEP to take responsibility for the grant objectives, coalitions have created appropriate structures to govern the work of their projects—to hire staff, oversee the planning and implementation activities, evaluate their success, and plan for the future. Each one has identified priority needs, created and implemented responsive solutions, advocated for systems change, and mobilized new resources to augment the existing system of assistance in their community. This has been done within the context of their unique community cultures and the guiding principles of BAIEP.

What have these community coalitions found and what solutions have they devised to tackle system problems? The issues that concern elders in BAIEP communities are not surprising: lack of information about options; language and cultural barriers to existing services; limited access to formal services such as in-home supportive services, adult protective services, and transportation; and need for support that has not existed, such as home repair, targeted (nontraditional) outreach, or peer counseling. Coalitions have made strategic decisions and designed projects to fill specific gaps that directly affect the daily lives of older adults, and to advocate for lasting changes to formal programs and policies.

Outreach based in the neighborhood, businesses, and churches; central telephone lines for information and emergency assistance; and culturally appropriate case management are examples of programs that have put isolated elders and their families in touch with appropriate services. Other needs have been met by creating programs run by and with volunteers, who provide information, visiting, counseling, driving, cooking, cleaning, home repair, and other services. Advocacy by community coalitions has changed paratransit delivery systems, modified meal programs to provide ethnic food, and reshaped funding priorities for elder programs.

Volunteers are at the heart of many coalition efforts to expand informal resources. BAIEP projects have been very successful in recruiting a sizable number of volunteers who had not previously been involved.

The funders of the BAIEP program are supporting an independent evaluation of the program now being conducted by Harder and Kibbe Research and Consulting. Initial findings indicate the following: "As the program grows and matures, important lessons are being learned about community-driven interventions built around an empowerment model which emphasizes consumer choice and systems change. . . . These services are having an important impact on the quality of life for older clients and their caregivers. By taking innovative approaches to outreach and community education, these programs are reaching many individuals who had been 'invisible' to the formal system of care."

*   *   *

Lori Andersen is the program coordinator of the Bay Area Independent Elders Program, San Francisco.

Chapter 16

Moving from Outdoor to Indoor Plumbing: Decreasing the Risk of Institutionalization Among Appalachian Elders*

William S. Hubbard, Rosemary Blieszner, and Jeffrey W. London

In a discussion of the critical link between housing conditions and health, Sargis and her colleagues (1987) stated that "badly constructed houses do for the healthy what bad hospitals do for the sick." Across the United States, rural elderly citizens occupy a disproportionate share of substandard housing (Krout, 1986). In Virginia, where one in three elders resides in a rural area (Cotter and Wich, 1989), 53,191 of a total of 2,000,096 year-round housing units for the entire population have no plumbing (Virginia Water Project, 1988). Living without indoor plumbing may not be a hardship for some, but negotiating the daily rituals of carrying and heating water and walking to and from outhouses is beyond the capabilities of many of Appalachia's frail elders (Hubbard, Blieszner and London, 1990) and has important implications for their health, well-being, and ability to remain at home.

*This research was supported by the Gerontological Society of America's 1990 Student Fellowship Program in Applied Gerontology with funding from the National Foundation on Gerontology. Expanded versions of the chapter have been presented as papers at the 1990 annual meeting of the Gerontological Society of American and at the 1991 annual meeting of the Southern Gerontological Society.

MODEL PROGRAM

Virginia Mountain Housing, Inc. (VMH), a nonprofit corporation based in Appalachian Virginia, provides safe and affordable housing to low-income Virginians. As a Gerontological Society of America student fellow, the first author joined forces with vmh to study the relationship of incomplete plumbing to the risk of institutionalization for elders in the counties of Montgomery and Giles. Of the 3,742 elder-owned houses in the two counties, nearly 500 were lacking complete indoor plumbing (Virginia Water Project, 1988). Plumbing deficits varied and included faulty waste removal systems, contaminated water sources, and, for some, no water sources for their houses. Our primary focus was the relationship of plumbing deficits to the risk of institutionalization for elders on VMH's assistance waiting list. Data were collected for VMH to use in seeking funding for a new indoor-plumbing installation program.

We interviewed 21 elders living with incomplete indoor plumbing and six of their family caregivers. Five elders who had recently received indoor plumbing provided by VMH assistance were interviewed to gain an understanding of whether and how the availability of indoor plumbing had affected their independence.

FINDINGS

Twenty of the 21 elders living without indoor plumbing and all six primary caregivers said they believed that plumbing deficits would eventually lead to premature or unnecessary institutionalization. All six caregivers said they believed that their relatives' plumbing deficits added to the stress of caregiving. All five elders with recently installed plumbing said they believed that indoor plumbing was critical to their independence. Characteristics of the respondents and the implications of living with incomplete indoor plumbing are provided in greater detail in Table 1.

From the eight health and human service providers interviewed during the pilot phase of the project, we learned that most physicians are unaware of plumbing deficits in the homes of their clients. This is unfortunate, because many elders discharged to homes with plumbing deficits have health conditions that cannot be properly cared for without adequate plumbing. Healthcare providers interviewed said they believed that readmissions to acute-care facilities were frequent for such individuals. The director of a local home healthcare agency asserted that plumbing deficits make home healthcare plans more costly to implement.

Table 1. Older Adults Living With Incomplete Indoor Plumbling (N = 21)
Demographic Characteristics and Implications

Demographic Characteristics	
Age	59 to 94
Gender[a]	
female	19
male	2
Marital Status[a]	
widowed	17
married	2
never married	2
Race[a]	
Caucasian	9
African American	2
Formal education (years)[b]	7
Annual income[b]	$5,704
Linited ADL/IADL functioning[a]	15
No source of running water at house[a]	5
Implications of Inadequate Plumbing	
Difficulty getting to outhouse[a]	
because of health problems	12
because of fear of falling	9
Had fallen during trups to the outhouse[a]	9
Had broken bones when falling during trips to the outhouse[a]	5
Felt unsafe carrying/heating water[a]	11
Believed that a plumbing deficit was a serious hardship[a]	20

[a] = frequency

[b] = mean

IN THEIR OWN WORDS

Allowing the respondents to speak for themselves can deepen our understanding of the intersection of incomplete plumbing and the risk of institutionalization. The following are some questions asked of respondents, and their answers:

Question: Do you think that your health is affected by living without indoor plumbing?

Answer: What would *you* do if you had to go out there on the back porch on a bucket in the cold?...[You] squat down and sometimes you don't know whether you're going to get up or not, or just fall down and lay out there until somebody finds you. It has happened to me. (59-year-old woman)

Q: Does not having indoor plumbing increase a person's chance of going to a nursing home prematurely?

A: But when I put him in the nursing home, I didn't promise to leave him there till a lifetime because, you know, after anybody lives together for 48 years it's not easy for one to stay in one place and one the other. . .and that's my main concern about a bathroom is gettin' him home. If I ever get a bathroom in this house, I am going to bring him home. I have almost decided to bring him home without one, but it would be hard—it would be hard on me now, I know, especially in the wintertime. (66-year-old spouse of an 82-year-old institutionalized man)

Q: Is it harder for you to take care of your relative because he does not have indoor plumbing?

A: Well, as I said before, there is never enough water when you have to carry it and then heat it. You can't do a good job, you know. His dishes are not nearly sanitary. (57-year-old female caregiver)

Q: How has having a bathroom affected your independence?

A: If it weren't for my new bathroom, I'm sure that I'd be in one of them [nursing] homes by now. (82-year-old woman with recently installed plumbing)

CONCLUSION

This project report has a happy ending. VMH received funding from the Commonwealth of Virginia, and after one year had installed plumbing in approximately 50 homes occupied by Appalachian elders. Funding was renewed, and more plumbing installations are occurring as of this writing.

ACKNOWLEDGMENT

For their invaluable support, the authors wish to thank the staffs of the Gerontological Society of America and Virginia Mountain Housing, Inc., and Stephanie Robinson, B.S.W.

*   *   *

William S. Hubbard, M.A., is an adjunct instructor in the Gerontology Programs at San Francisco State University and a doctoral candidate in the Department of Family and Child Development, Virginia Polytechnic Institute and State University, Blacksburg. Rosemary Blieszner, Ph.D., is an associate professor, Department of Family and Child Development, and associate director of the Center for Gerontology, both at Virginia Polytechnic Institute and State University. Jeffrey W. London, M.S., is executive director, Mountain Shelter, Inc., Wytheville, Va.

REFERENCES

Cotter, J. J. and Wich, N., 1989. *Virginia's Rural Elderly—What Do They Need? Results of a Preliminary Survey of Human Service Agencies.* Richmond, Va.: Virginia Department for the Aging.

Hubbard, W. S., Blieszner, R. and London, J. W., 1990. "Without Indoor Plumbing in Appalachia: Issues of Health, Independence, Caregiving and Care Receiving in Late Life." Paper presented at the 43rd annual scientific meeting of the Gerontological Society of America, Boston.

Krout, J. A., 1986. *The Aged in Rural America.* Westport, Conn.: Greenwood Press.

Sargis, N. M., Jennrich, J. A. and Murray, K. M., 1987. "Housing Conditions and Health: A Crucial Link." *Nursing and Health Care* 8(6): 335–38.

Virginia Water Project, 1988. *Water for Tomorrow: A Report on Water and Wastewater Needs in Virginia.* Roanoke, Va.: Gurtner Printing Co.

Chapter 17

Neighborhoods That Make Sense: Community Allies for Elders Aging in Place

Patrick Cullinane

In an interview with Bill Moyers (1989), Robert Bellah, author of *Habits of the Heart* and *The Good Society*, said, "We can only solve our problems through the tough process of becoming involved in our neighborhoods, in our local communities. . . ." In order to become involved, Bellah asserts, we must be attentive to the world around us. For just as children flourish under attentive parents and students under attentive teachers, our places can make more sense if, with our neighbors, we pay attention to our place, the people in it, and how it works for all of us.

Today, if we take the time to see who our neighbor is, who is using our business, who joins us at club meetings, who sits next to us in church, it will be apparent that our world is growing older. Bellah's admonition to be attentive is critical if we are to secure hospitable places for our parents, for our older relatives and friends of today, and for succeeding generations, including our own. Like helpful grocery store clerks, some of our best allies for this endeavor may be with us every day.

The authors of the other chapters in this volume describe with eloquence and authority the impact of the phenomenon of aging in place on our formal service systems and the accompanying challenges and options. America is confronted with a large number of citizens who, in their retirement and their continued aging, will place demands upon and be resources for all sectors of society.

Popular media show how people are becoming aware of the importance of place to our aging America. An architectural writer in the article, "Our Elders, Ourselves: Toward a New Community Vision," in *Metropolitan Home* asks the question, "Where will our aging parents live?" (Flanagan, 1991). The *Wall Street Journal* chronicles the challenges rural elders face in "Iowa Towns Shrivel As the Young People Head for the Cities," leaving elders behind (Shribman, 1991).

No one questions the need (it has been well documented) for an expanded formal system to enable elders to age well and safely in place. What is also needed, however, is an understanding by people at the neighborhood or community level of just what they can do for elders, expecially those at risk. We in the field of aging need to focus our efforts beyond the traditional aging network and make allies of all kinds of organizations and businesses that have not previously put the needs of at-risk elders on their agendas. Their involvement is essential to generating caring communities with and for older people.

We need to help our neighbors to stop and pay attention to their everyday lives and recognize that, consciously and unconsciously, we all play an important role in each other's lives—a role that helps define the quality of living in our community, how hospitable a place it is, and whether it is a good place in which to grow old.

ASA's Aging in the Neighborhood Project is one piece of the national response to this need. It is part of the Administration on Aging's (AoA) National Eldercare Campaign, which reflects AoA's belief that we are poorly prepared as a nation to respond to an America aging in place. In their judgment, the country's level of awareness, knowledge, and sensitivity is neither adequate nor appropriate for the decision making that lies ahead. In the neighborhood project, we have reached out to new national audiences. Through a national conference, presentations, articles in *Aging Today* and other publications, Spring 1992 issue of *Generations*, and an educational videotape, "A Good Place to Grow Old," hosted by Charles Osgood of CBS News, we are attempting to expand awareness of and participation in the dialogue about how we can create hospitable places with and for our older citizens.

In this effort, we have drawn upon several excellent examples. The Andrus Gerontology Center's Project LINC (Living Independently through Neighborhood Cooperation) is one. It focused on "friends, neighbors, clergy, storekeepers, bartenders, and others who might be labeled 'just plain citizens'... as an informal circle of helpers for a person experiencing problems." The project found that "providing non-institutional long-term care on a neighborhood basis was an effective way of serving the elderly." Project LINC's final report (Kaplan, 1982) presents these lessons and others learned about organizational principles and participant benefits. It serves as a very useful guide to others wanting to engage and empower communities on behalf of members in need.

Another example is the Bay Area Independent Elders Project. In her chapter in this volume, Lori Andersen shares the experiences of a variety of programs that are linking the "nontraditional" network with the formal aging network. In one program, a social worker walks a "beat" in an inner city neighborhood. Through her contacts with merchants, bankers, pharmacists, and barbers, the social worker and the resources she represents become known to the community. In turn, she gains the confidence of the merchants, who refer their customers who need her assistance in maintaining independence.

The spiritual community plays a pivotal role in the life of a neighborhood, and in elders' lives. There are over 340,000 congregations in the United States, and about 40 percent of elders identify themselves with one of them (Moyers, 1989). Congregations not only represent the heart and conscience of a community but also an enduring, intergenerational social structure (Fahey, 1991).

The Robert Wood Johnson Foundation's Interfaith Volunteer Caregivers demonstration has grown into a movement. The Neighboring Shepherd's program of the Shepherd's Center in Greensboro, North Carolina, is one example. Volunteers stay alert to the needs of older adults living nearby. They have reached 15 neighborhoods and 3,200 homes. There are over 200 Neighboring Shepherd volunteers in place, linked to the local aging network.

Under the leadership of Elbert Cole, the Consumer Health Information Research Institute in Kansas City, Missouri, has established a Congregation Resource Center. One center project is to assist the local public administrator with ward-protectees. Forty-three trained volunteers from eight congregations visit 142 people who are ward-protectees and file written status reports with the administrator. The program greatly expands the resources of the administrator for a population that tends to be friendless and isolated.

The public schools in Colorado's Littleton and Douglas County operate a senior citizen tax rebate program. Older homeowners are given the opportunity to work for the district and receive rebates on their school property taxes. Participants do everything from working in classrooms, clinics, and the cafeteria, to helping on the playground, in computer labs, in the print shop or the library. The program has generated goodwill and increased understanding between schools and the community.

The Wal-Mart Corporation has undertaken innovative measures in response to an older customer base—wider aisles, seating and waiting areas throughout their stores, large-print signs, older customers' preferred products stocked on well-lighted shelves within easy reach. According to Margaret Wylde (1991) of the Institute for Technology Development, "the changes they first made as a philanthropic effort were not only beneficial to the recipient but to other market segments—not to mention the bottom line."

Action for Boston Community Development, Inc., has designed the How-To-Do-It Kit for Elder Housing Planning. The kit helps communities investigate, evaluate, and implement with their elders housing and housing-related services to allow choices of aging in place or moving into a more appropriate new home. The kit is described as an effective tool to help neighborhoods respond in a way that neither pits the generations against each other nor "ghettoizes" elders. Such an approach seems like an appropriate way to address the growing question of how to maintain the quality of the housing stock and prevent deterioration of the neighborhood often associated with poorly maintained housing and lower property values (Wekerle, 1985).

In March of 1992, the Home Builders Association of Maryland, with Hechinger Company and the Maryland Office on Aging, initiated a statewide home repair program, "Senior Hospitality," for low-income elders. Materials and skills were donated to improve homes with regard to safety and security, energy conservation, and interior and exterior work. Comparable efforts have been started around the country in the Christmas in April program.

No sample listing of community responses to link the informal with the formal would be adequate unless it included the Gatekeeper programs initiated in 1978 by the Puget Sound Power and Light Company of Washington state. These programs demonstrate how as part of their regular jobs employees can be trained to recognize elders in need of assistance. The programs represent a successful linkage of the public and private sectors to maintain or promote hospitable places for at-risk elders. According to the AARP (Hexter, 1989), there are at least 173 utility companies with similar programs in 46 states and the District of Columbia.

The country's numerous civic clubs also are resources for creating more hospitable places. The Rotary International, for example, has a Committee for Service to the Elderly, and Kiwanis International has as its stated purpose "service to youth and the elderly, to community and nation."

All of the foregoing highlight some of the allies the aging network has in promoting caring communities for our growing number of elders aging in place. Included among these allies are elders themselves. A study of volunteerism by Marriott Corporation (1991) and AoA found 1.5 million older people volunteering across the country, with another 14.1 million waiting to be asked. ASA's Aging in the Neighborhoods Project will continue to share these experiences with its target audience in the hope that others will take up the challenge and seize the opportunity to make their communities, their neighborhoods, good places to grow old.

As part of this effort, ASA will be publishing a compendium of resources identifying model and innovative community programs involving business, labor, volunteer, education, and faith communities in responding to the needs of at-risk elders. If you have programs to recommend, please let us know.

*　　*　　*

Patrick Cullinane, M.S., is director of the American Society on Aging's "Aging in the Neighborhood Project," San Francisco.

REFERENCES

Fahey, C. F., 1991. "Linking Meaning and Social Service: The Role of Religious Groups." *Aging Today* (June–July): 11–12.

Flanagan, B., 1991. "Our Elders, Ourselves: Toward a New Community Vision." *Metropolitan Home* (January): 34–36.

Hexter, 1989. "Private Sector Services to Aid Older Americans: A Survey of Gatekeeper Programs and Other Programs Sponsored by Utility Companies." Cleveland, Ohio: American Association of Retired Persons.

Kaplan, B., 1982. *Project linc Manual: Living Independently Through Neighborhood Cooperation.* Los Angeles: Institute for Policy and Program Development, Andrus Gerontology Center, University of Southern California.

Marriott Corporation, 1991. *Marriott Senior Volunteerism Study.* Washington, D.C.

Moyers, B., 1989. *A World of Ideas.* New York: Doubleday.

Shribman, D., 1991. "Iowa Towns Shrivel As the Young People Head for the Cities." *Wall Street Journal,* April 24: A1, A9.

Wekerle, G., 1985. "From Refuge to Service Center: Neighborhoods That Support Women." *Sociological Focus* 18 (2): 79–95.

Wylde, M., 1991. "Business in Tomorrow's Neighborhoods: Serving Many Generations." *Aging Today* (June–July): 10.

Chapter 18

With Elders in Mind*

Mary Sit

Eighty-two-year-old Gunnar Dybwad spent $34,000 in order to finish out his life at home.

Seven years ago, the retired professor of social work and his researcher wife, Rosemary, renovated their two-story Wellesley, Massachusetts, house to make it easier to age in place. "It's our anti-nursing-home insurance," explained Dybwad.

The couple converted a back porch into a bedroom, added a bathroom—all adjoining a deck that is two-thirds covered by a skylight. The downstairs suite serves as guest quarters for overnight visitors, but in the future, if either Dybwad or his 81-year-old wife finds it difficult to climb the stairs to the other bedrooms, the first floor will function as a self-contained unit.

Both the guest room and bathroom are completely accessible to wheelchairs. The bathroom is equipped with special grab bars by the toilet and tub. The deck includes a railing that can be removed and replaced with a hydraulic lift.

Most elders resist the idea of renovating their house to make it more comfortable as they age—especially those who are completely mobile and in good health. "It's the first tangible expression of their aging, and often that's a shocking thing they have to contemplate," said Richard Duncan, associate director of the Adaptive Environment Center in Boston, a nonprofit firm specializing in creating barrier-free designs.

*Mary Sit is on the staff of the Boston Globe, in which this chapter originally appeared. It is reprinted with permission.

Dybwad, who has studied architectural planning and disabilities, said it is only sensible to make changes before disaster strikes.

"We changed our house in order to be ready," he said, adding that the renovations took nine months to complete. "We want to die here."

In 1990, elders age 65 and older numbered 31.6 million—12.6 percent of the U.S. population, according to the American Association of Retired Persons. "Five to 10 percent of those between 65 and 75—but more than one-third of those 85 and older, the fastest growing segment of the population—need assistance in one or more basic activities of life: dressing, bathing, eating, walking, shopping," said Irving K. Zola, a professor of sociology at Brandeis University, who specializes in aging issues.

Creating a comfortable environment no longer means duplicating a hospital room. Products on the market now come in fashionable colors and sleek designs.

Jacqueline B. Dobson, an occupational therapist and president of Solutions for Accessibility in Framingham, Massachusetts, has advised clients for the past eight years on how to adapt their homes to easier living. Here is her prescription for creating a comfortable environment.

The kitchen. Replace double round faucet controls with a single lever control. Install organizational bins you can pull out to avoid reaching down and in. Place a spice rack under the upper cabinet. Use a knife with a handle perpendicular to the blade to avoid joint strain.

The bathroom. Replace towel racks with securely mounted grab bars one and one-fourth inches in diameter and not more than one and one-half inches from the wall. If you cannot get into the tiled wall area above the tub, install clamp-on style grab bars. Consider a hand-held shower head, shower seat, and nonslip tub surface. Use soap-on-a-rope to prevent trying to retrieve slippery bars that slide to the drain.

Environmental controls. Most environmental control devices cost less than $200. For those who have trouble recalling phone numbers, try a big button picture phone. Simply press a button with the party's picture mounted on the button, and the number is automatically dialed. Or there is the phone where you merely pick up the receiver and speak the party's name to automatically dial the party's number.

An automatic stove turn-off device shuts off the stove after a preset time. Remote transmitters can turn on and off up to 16 electronic devices such as lamps, fans, radios.

If an older person is hard of hearing, he or she can use a device that causes a lamp to flash when the phone rings. Light switches that illuminate in the dark make middle-of-the-night trips to the bathroom safer.

While elders may balk at installing items that clearly indicate special needs due to aging, many of the changes are simply a safety issue, said Duncan of the Adaptive Environment Center.

The very same features that make it easier for an elder to get around also make it simpler for a five-year-old. "It's truly an issue that crosses all age spans," said Duncan.

For example, replacing doorknobs with levers that push down make opening doors easy for children and for elders who may suffer from arthritis, Duncan points out.

Diana Abrachkin, a 42-year-old architect and owner of Architectural Design and Consulting in Lincoln, Massachusetts, said she will only build structures that are completely accessible. "In the future, accessibility will be considered a virtue in the home—just like a Jacuzzi," she said.

Architects who adopt a holistic approach to the design process— creating aesthetically pleasing designs that work both for the abled and disabled—said it is important to strike a balance that is visually acceptable by people who are not impaired.

"Does it become an integral part of the architecture, or does it look like it's bastardized and adapted? That's what you don't want," said Joseph Del Vecchio, an architect who uses a wheelchair and who owns Access Development Group in East Providence, Rhode Island.